CASE STUDIES IN EDUCATION AND CULTURE

General Editors
GEORGE *and* LOUISE SPINDLER
Stanford University

INDIAN EDUCATION IN THE CHIAPAS HIGHLANDS

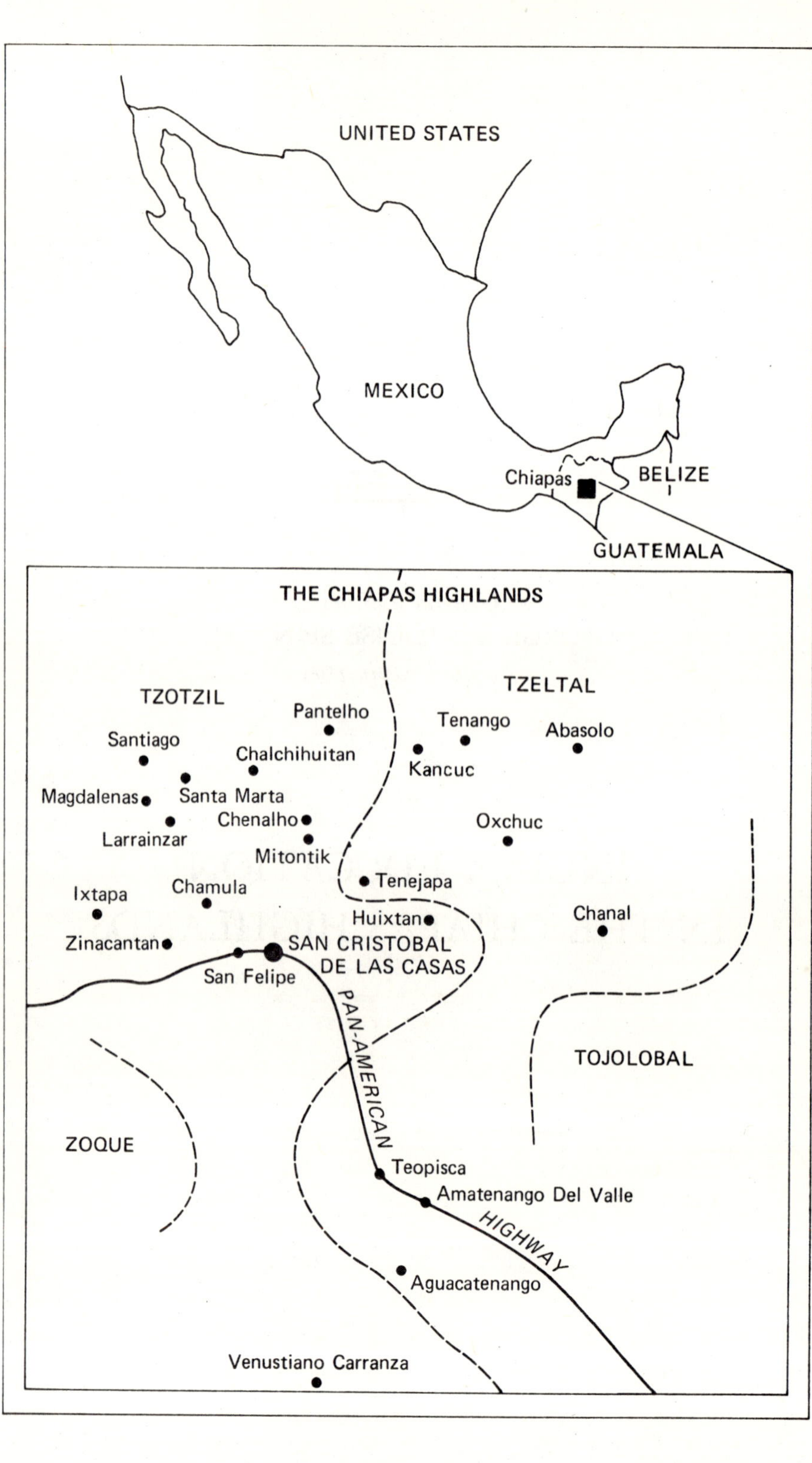
UNITED STATES
MEXICO
Chiapas
BELIZE
GUATEMALA
THE CHIAPAS HIGHLANDS
TZOTZIL
TZELTAL
Pantelho
Tenango
Abasolo
Santiago
Chalchihuitan
Kancuc
Magdalenas
Santa Marta
Chenalho
Oxchuc
Larrainzar
Mitontik
Ixtapa
Chamula
Tenejapa
Chanal
Huixtan
Zinacantan
SAN CRISTOBAL
DE LAS CASAS
San Felipe
PAN-AMERICAN
TOJOLOBAL
ZOQUE
Teopisca
Amatenango Del Valle
HIGHWAY
Aguacatenango
Venustiano Carranza

INDIAN EDUCATION IN THE CHIAPAS HIGHLANDS

NANCY MODIANO
The Catholic University of America

HOLT, RINEHART AND WINSTON, INC.
New York • Chicago • San Francisco • Atlanta
Dallas • Montreal • Toronto • London • Sydney

This study is dedicated to my parents
Albert and Eva Modiano
and
to the Indians of the Highlands and all others
who struggle to make sense of our modern world

Library of Congress Cataloging in Publication Data

Modiano, Nancy
Indian education in the Chiapas highlands.

(Case studies in education and culture)
Bibliography: p. 143
1. Indians of Mexico—Education. 2. Indians of
Mexico—Children. 3. Indians of Mexico—Chiapas.
I. Title. II. Series
F1219.3.E3M62 371.9'7'970727 72–13905
ISBN: 0—03—084237—9

Foreword

ABOUT THE SERIES

This series brings to students the results of direct observation and participation in educational process, by anthropologists, in a variety of cultural settings, including some within the contemporary United States. Each of the books in this series is selected as an enduring example of educational anthropology. Classrooms, schools, communities and their schools, cultural transmission in societies where there are no schools in the Western sense, all are represented in the series. The authors of these studies move beyond formalistic treatments of institutions to the interaction among the people engaged in educative events, their thinking and feeling, and to the educative transactions themselves.

Education is a cultural process. Every act of teaching and learning is a cultural event. Education recruits new members into society and maintains the culture. Education may also be an instrument for change as new adaptations are disseminated.

Generalizations about relationships between schools and communities, education and society, and education and culture become meaningful when education is studied as a cultural process. This series is intended for use in courses in education, and in anthropology and the other social sciences, where these relationships are particularly relevant. They will stimulate thinking and discussion about education that is not confined by one's own cultural experience. The crosscultural emphasis of the series is particularly significant. Without this perspective, our view will be obscured by ethnocentric bias.

ABOUT THE AUTHOR

Nancy Modiano is Associate Professor of Education at the Catholic University of America in Washington, D.C., where she teaches courses in educational anthropology as well as in curriculum. She received all her formal education at New York University, where she also held appointments as Instructor and Assistant Professor. She first went to Chiapas in 1958 as a tourist and immediately saw the intriguing educational implications inherent in comparing the bilingual programs in some of the Indian schools with the all-Spanish programs in others. A series of almost yearly pilot studies led to a doctoral dissertation (supported in part by the U.S. Office of Education and in part by an Ida M. Bowman scholarship); that study has become a standard reference for bilingual education. She has continued to visit Chiapas frequently and has done further fieldwork to amplify aspects of the dissertation, resulting in this case study. She has also participated in a study of rural Mexican mestizos and is currently working with Black inner-city children.

ABOUT THE BOOK

This case study, like those by Alan Peshkin on the Kanuri and Bruce Grindal on the Sisala, is about the use of formal education as an agent of economic development and social change. It is a particularly revelant case study for educators, social scientists, and students in the United States, not only because the Indians in the Chiapas Highlands of Mexico are in close geographic proximity, but also because the situation of the Indians in Mexico is similar to that of many minority groups in our country. The Indians of Chiapas live in *municipios* largely divorced from the dominant non-Indian population of Mexico and its urban centers. Although Indians constitute approximately 10 percent of the total population of Mexico, their way of life has been characterized by social and cultural isolation, nonliteracy, and economic disadvantage. Paradoxically, however, they represent the most visible continuity with the civilizations of the Mayans and Aztecs, who, with others in varying degrees like them, were the original inhabitants and possessors of the land. The struggle to acculturate and eventually to assimilate the Indian population into that of Mexico as a whole is therefore of long standing, beginning in fact when the first Conquistadors arrived. The educational programs fostered by the government of Mexico, however, are designed not only to acculturate and assimilate the Indians, but also to improve their social, economic, and political situation. The consequences of such attempts in Mexico and elsewhere in the world where education is used as an agent for change are problematic.

There are many parallels to schools for minorities in the United States. The educational materials available are often inappropriate to the children's needs or background. For example, the case study mentions a federal school in which the first reading lesson after the introduction of vowels is about a teddy bear. Few Highland Chiapas Indians have any notion about furry toy bears. In the second grade reading program the author observed the children reading a story about "the mailman." The story began with a large colored picture of a street scene, showing the mailman in a mestizo village. Such nonrelatedness of curricular content is made even more irrelevant to the students' progress due to a second set of circumstances, ritualized methods of teaching. Children are expected to digest a book page by page, memorizing as they go along, a process considered identical to learning. This contrasts sharply with the Indian concepts of learning and mastering, of "becoming accustomed" through the performance of real adult tasks. As one informant pointed out, perhaps the children are so confused in school that they do not know what else to do other than memorize.

The situation is made worse, particularly in the federal schools, by the use of Spanish as the major language of instruction rather than as a second language to be learned. Together with the minimal modifications of curriculum made for the Indian cultural background and rural situation, the use of Spanish tends to put comprehension of the subject matter beyond the children's reach.

Dr. Modiano was fortunate in being able to study schools that varied considerably with respect to the emphasis upon utilization of Spanish in the curriculum, either as the major language of instruction or as a second language. As she explains, these differences are due to the varying histories of specific schools: Some of them were established by the National Indian Institute, founded in 1948, while the federal and state schools are part of an older system designed for Spanish-speaking mestizos. The former have been more explicitly directed toward assimilation and have made relatively more adaptation to the characteristics and needs of the local Indian cultures. The author collected test data on reading comprehension to determine the relative effectiveness of the all-Spanish versus the bilingual approach. The results of her study, which is considered a classic in bilingual education and is continually cited, correspond to those obtained in other countries where the same situation prevails. The bilingual approach produced better reading comprehension in Spanish; in the last chapter she deals with some of the reasons why this is so.

The case study as a whole is well-rounded, beginning with a chapter on the existing Indian culture and its history. Against this background, she examines early, middle, and later childhood. This section alone could constitute a case study. She makes the book particularly meaningful, however, by her attention to the schools and their effectiveness. The reader has a rare opportunity to see the relatedness and nonrelatedness of the schools, the children, and their cultural and community background.

George and Louise Spindler
General Editors
STANFORD, CALIFORNIA

Acknowledgments

This investigation was supported in part by a Small Contract (Project S–237) from the U.S. Office of Education, Cooperative Research Branch, in part by an Ida M. Bowman Scholarship awarded by New York University School of Education, and in part by a New York University Institutional Grant.

There are two Chiapas Indians to whom I am especially indebted; since I do not know whom to put first, I will do so in alphabetical order. Jacinto Arias Sojob, who gathered much of the biographical material, opened new perspectives for me with his profound insights. Salvador Lopez Calixto was my assistant during much of the fieldwork; without his loyalty, sensitivity, and many talents, the execution of the study would have been infinitely more difficult.

I would also like to thank Professors H. Harry Giles, George Manolakes, and Milton Schwebel, who guided me past the many pitfalls of my doctoral dissertation, which forms a part of this book. Nathan Jaspen helped clarify the statistical design. Professors Fidencio Montes Sanchez and Evangelina Arana de Swadesh introduced me to the life of the Highland Indians and helped me with the translations of the group reading tests. Marcelina Jiminez and Esperanza Lozada supplied most of the pictures for the group test. Gertrude Duby de Blom was ever available to help unravel problems of field travel. Professor Jorge Estrada greatly facilitated the gathering of data in Mexico City. I wish to express my heartfelt gratitude to all of them.

The late Professor Julio de la Fuente of Mexico's National Indian Institute aided immensely in the execution of the field study, yet never tried to influence its course or results. To him I am truly indebted.

To the teachers and students of the Chiapas Highlands, I owe my gratitude for their generous hospitality and patience.

All of these and the host of others, colleagues, friends, and students, who are not mentioned here, I acknowledge with heartfelt thanks.

N. M.

Contents

1 / Introduction

This is a case study in Indian education, both formal and informal, in the Highlands of Chiapas, Mexico. Indians, speaking fifty major indigenous languages,[1] comprise slightly over 10 percent of Mexico's population. As in many countries of the world, the national leaders have turned to formal education to lay the groundwork for major economic development and social change. They see in formal schooling the means for incorporating the Indian minorities into the national life.

The state of Chiapas lies at one end of Mexico and borders on both Guatemala and the Pacific Ocean. San Cristobal de Las Casas, the economic and political center of the Highlands, sits in a valley about 7000 feet above sea level, while the surrounding Indian communities are located at between 4500 and 8500 feet above sea level. Due to the altitude the climate is temperate, but frosts are common during the winter nights in the higher sections. Rainfall is abundant, averaging about 45 inches a year in San Cristobal. Much of the area was once covered by a temperate forest, with large tracts of evergreens, orchids, ferns, mosses, and bromeliads at the highest reaches and a deciduous tropical forest on the sheltered slopes below. Apparently these forests were once rich in wildlife such as deer, rabbit, and several species of fox and cat, but most have been hunted off by now as more and more subsistence farm plots (*milpas*) have been cleared. Squirrels, opossums, and skunks are still found occasionally, but only small birds abound (Vogt 1969:6–8).

Two distinct ethnic groups inhabit the Highlands today, *ladinos* (local mestizos) and Indians, with the latter subdivided into over twenty tribes.[2] Indians outnumber the ladinos by a ratio of about 7:1 (at least 220,000 Indians to perhaps 30,000 ladinos).

Although the Indian *municipios* (municipalities or tribal regions with recognized

---

[1] The word Indian denotes a native speaker of an indigenous meso-American language. This is the official criteria for distinguishing Indians from other Mexicans and has been in effect since at least the 1960 census. All other official criteria are also cultural and have been in effect at least since 1940 (See Caso 1958).

[2] These tribes include the *municipios* (municipalities) of Amatenango, Carranza, Chalchihuitan, Chamula, Chanal, Chenalho, Huixtan, Larrainzar, Mitontik, Oxchuc, Pantelho, San Felipe, Tenejapa, and Zinacantan, as well as the smaller tribes (*agencias municipales*) of Abasolo, Aguacatenango, Kancuc, Magdalenas, San Sebastian, Santa Caterina, Santa Marta, Tenango, and Villa de Las Rosas.

The river at Abasolo.

geographic and political boundaries) border upon one another and many Indian municipios contain small pockets of ladinos (just as some Indians live within the boundaries of San Cristobal), contacts among the groups are limited almost entirely to the economic sphere. Indians supply agricultural products and occasional manual labor to the ladinos and occasionally to other tribes, while ladinos supply trade goods manufactured locally or brought in from other parts of Mexico.

HISTORY OF THE REGION

The Highlands area appears to have been first settled about 500 A.D. by peoples moving up from the lowland jungles. They lived in easily defensible positions, especially hilltops, which they crowned with platform mounds to serve as centers for religious activities. From these mounds there descended a series of crude masonry terraces, some of which may also have held smaller mounds for religious activities. It is here that the principle functionaries probably lived, while the common people lived below, closer to their fields (Vogt 1969:13–14). By 1000 A.D., these headlands appear to have been abandoned in favor of the valleys, although they are still remembered in some of the legends as holy places, the homes of the oldest gods and of people's souls (Vogt 1969:15).

Each of the tribes has its own tales of a religious past. The Chamulas revere Tzontevitz, their highest peak, as the home of the older and more powerful Totikshun, or Ch'ultotik, their principle deity. The Zinacantecos consider Kalvario, a peak close to their religious center, as the holiest of places, and they have crowned it with crosses set in crude masonry platforms. There is a peak on the edge of Amatenango where it is believed that the souls of the people live; it, too, is crowned with a cross set in a crude masonry platform. The patron saint of Oxchuc is known far and wide as the savior of humanity and the giver of rains. There is a story told of how he came, accompanied by the ancestors of present-day Oxchuqueros, to choose his present home.

> This is the story of the ancient Saint Thomas. He came from a place that they call Guatemala, in search of the navel of the Earth. He was always accompanied by a serpent and many followers. When the serpent raised its head, it was a sign that they had not yet found the navel of the Earth, that they had to move on. They came to a place named Chanal and built some houses and a chapel there. But the serpent raised its head and they had to go further. They came to a place they called Paixac. There, too, they built some houses and a church, but the serpent raised its head again; they had not found the navel of the Earth. They went on to a place called Hermitewitz and again they built houses and a church. Again the serpent raised its head; Saint Thomas thought that they had better continue their search, for they had not yet found the navel of the Earth.
>
> This time they went even further, perhaps 40 or 45 kilometers, and came to a place called Ocosingo. Here they built many houses and a big church. But the serpent slithered on, dragging its body along the earth and raising its head, which meant that they had not yet found the navel of the Earth.
>
> Saint Thomas said, "We must leave immediately. Let's see where we shall go." They always followed the serpent. When it pointed to the east they went toward the east; when it pointed to the west, they went toward the west. If it pointed to the north they moved northward. This time it pointed to the west, and Saint Thomas said, "We must leave." But his wife, the Virgin of Candelaria, thought, "No, I'm not going. We've traveled far. We've traveled a long, long time. I'm not going; I'm going to stay here. I like it here, even if the serpent doesn't." And to this day that is where she is, in Ocosingo.
>
> Saint Thomas said, "You may stay here. Take care of yourself. But I have to move on; I have to go with the serpent." Saint Thomas and all his helpers went on until they came to a place that is called Pohiltik. They thought at last that they had found the navel of the Earth. They began to work. They built many houses and a big church. All of a sudden the serpent raised its head again, pointing to the north. "Well, we'll have to leave," said Saint Thomas.
>
> At last the serpent rested at a place called Karowitz. They built a church there, and there the serpent slept . . . for perhaps an hour. But again it raised its head, this time pointing to the south. It moved very slowly. "Well, we'll have to move on, but we're close to the navel of the Earth. We'll be there soon." When the serpent moved quickly that meant that they still had a long distance to

travel, but now it was moving very slowly. It stopped at a place called Yasnichin, which means the place where everybody gets water. There the serpent dived into the water.

"What shall we do now? The serpent hasn't told us anything," said the helpers.

Then the serpent spoke. "Now, by my orders, you may build your church. Saint Thomas shall be your patron in this place. And you, who have labored hard, shall live here all of your lives. You shall never have to tear down your work again. I shall remain here, for here is the navel of the Earth. Many peoples shall come, from many places, and gather here; they shall come on pilgrimages, so that Saint Thomas may order the rains for your plantings."

To this day people continue arriving on the pilgrimages, some from very far away, and that is how Oxchuc was formed.

Pilgrims still come to Oxchuc at the beginning of the rainy season, some hiking as many as five days to reach their patron. At night they play their music and dance in the town square. In the morning they pray and dance in the churchyard to honor the Saint before departing for home. Throughout the area people still pray to certain mountains and caves, knowing that they are speaking to the oldest of their gods.

Even now it appears that the settlement patterns and political structures that developed at the beginning of this millenium, when the people first settled in the valleys, have remained essentially the same. The area then, as now, was relatively isolated from the rest of the world; contacts were few with central Mexico, the Yucatan, or the Guatemala Highlands (Vogt 1969:14–16).

In 1519 the Spanish reached Yucatan and four years later the Chiapas Highlands were "discovered." It took another five years for the area to be subdued, due as much to the Spaniards' relative disinterest, compared to their energy in capturing the Aztec lands, as to the Indians' resistance. As in central Mexico, intertribal rivalries caused them to play into the hands of the Spanish and helped them, under the leadership of Diego de Mazariegos, establish peace (Vogt 1969:16–17). By 1536 forty Spaniards were living in Villa Real (later renamed San Cristobal) and others could be found on their estates or *encomiendas* (Remesal 1908:21), where they held the Indians as virtual slaves, extracting from them both tribute and labor. The encomienda of Chamula was given to Bernal Diaz del Castillo, the great chronicler of the conquest (Vogt 1969:17).

In 1544 Bishop Bartolomé de Las Casas arrived in Villa Real and, with the help of seventeen Dominican friars, set about converting the Indians and trying to improve their lot. For his efforts he won the undying enmity of the Spanish colonizers, but also some grudging cooperation. His greatest contribution to the Indians' welfare may have been the Law of the Indies, reinforced by Papal decree, which recognized the souls of catholicized Indians and, therefore, their status as human beings with rights to marry, keep their families intact, and partake of the sacraments.

In 1540 the King of Spain decreed, largely through Las Casas' instigation, that the Indians should be settled into towns, primarily to speed their acculturation, especially their religious conversion. Within seven or eight years after their arrival most of the churches standing today were built (Remesal 1908:52). The Dominican friars created towns as they spread the gospel, but as they moved on the newly created towns emptied, the people scattering to their former homes among the cornfields. This pre-Columbian pattern of empty towns which serve as religious-political and commercial centers predominates today throughout most of the Highlands (Vogt 1969:23).

In 1720 the encomiendas were officially abolished and gradually converted into haciendas; seldom did the land revert to the Indians. Peonage continued in the form of *baldaje*, a system under which Indians resident on the haciendas were required to give up to four days a week of free labor to the hacienda, in return for a house site and small milpa. In 1877 there were 528 haciendas in the Highlands; by 1910, after the implementation of the Ley Lerdo, which provided for the distribution of church lands, there were 1076 (Vogt 1969:19).

There were only two major Indian revolts from the time of the conquest until the Revolution of 1910. Both had strong religious overtones, with godlike figures serving as the rallying points for thousands of Indians who armed themselves and marched against the ladinos, pillaging as they went. Soldiers were called upon to quell both uprisings and the rebellions were quickly crushed. In 1712 the Tzeltals, accompanied by several Tzotzil tribes, revolted. Their movement centered in Kancuc, around the figure of a Virgin Mary who spoke through the person of a young Indian girl. In 1869 to 1870 the Chamulas began worshipping clay idols of their own making in preference to the ladino idols (wooden saints) in the church. They crucified a youth so that they could have a Christ of their own. Cuzcat was their leader, the priest their principal opponent. Like the previous rebellion in 1712, this one was quickly subdued (Vogt 1969:21–22). To this day fears of further Indian uprisings persist among the ladinos of San Cristobal.

* Since its founding in 1528, San Cristobal has maintained a somewhat feudal structure, with a minority of ladinos maintaining political and economic control over a majority of Indians. The ladino oligarchy has always been politically conservative, favoring strong local control rather than federal control and rarely granting Indians their civil, political, or economic rights without stiff resistance. Although lands were to be redistributed to the landless following the Revolution of 1910, it was not until the Cardenas regime of the late 1930s that the Indians began to recover their ancestral lands. Since 1952, the National Indian Institute (INI) has helped further the process.

The following story tells of the difficulties encountered along the way.

In 1954, Marcelo Santis Lopez, an Oxchuc Indian, then aged 18, was sent by the INI both to free from baldaje some people living just outside the border of Oxchuc and to establish a school for them. The *baldíos* (persons living in baldaje) came from five *fincas* (haciendas), the properties of a priest, three ladino merchants, and a Huistecan Indian.

The Huistecan had promised a site for the school, but instead complained to the judicial authorities in San Cristobal that an attempt was being made to steal his land. Marcelo won that court battle, just as he won all the subsequent ones, but the baldíos had to pay 400 *pesos* for a small piece of land that had originally cost 6! While the men constructed the schoolhouse, Marcelo taught his classes under the trees.

The finca owners continued their opposition, making at least two attempts on Marcelo's life. One evening he was sitting in his cooking shack teaching some little boys to read when he saw a flash of light. He blew out the candle and told the boys to shout that they were armed. Several parents heard the noise and came running. Later, when they went out to inspect the grounds, they found the prints of several sandals and three horses in the fresh mud. They also found a knife belonging to the Huistecan. The Oxchuqueros took the case to court and the Huistecan was jailed and fined.

Marcelo was accustomed to bathing every evening in a nearby stream. One evening as he was bathing he heard some children shout that men had entered his kitchen; they were carrying rifles. When Marcelo got close to the kitchen he saw from their tracks that they had gone into the woods. They were standing behind some trees, pointing their rifles at him. He ran to the kitchen, locked himself inside, and began to shout for help. Two men came, one of them armed with a musket. When Marcelo proposed that they go out to talk to the would-be assassins, the baldíos hung back. As others began to arrive the attackers retreated to a large clump of grass and then disappeared into the woods. Again Marcelo went to court.

The Huistecan then threatened his baldíos, claiming that he would throw them off his property. An Oxchuquero living in the vicinity offered a piece of land for the schoolhouse if only his children could attend. The baldíos decided to move their school, but their owners still did not leave them in peace. The Huistecan finca owner was the most impatient; the others assumed that in time Marcelo would fail and their baldíos would quiet down. At the same time they kept up the pressure against Marcelo, constantly threatening him. But by now he had begun to lose his fear.

Once more they sent men to kill him. This time Marcelo went out unarmed to meet them, daring them to come out of the woods and face him directly. They shot but missed. Some parents, who were watching from the kitchen, fired into the air, and again the would-be killers fled.

One of the ladinos, seeing that he no longer had any laborers to work for him, offered to sell his finca for 3000 pesos. The more the owners threatened, the more Marcelo urged the baldíos to somehow scrape together the money and buy it. It took four years to complete the payment of 3000 pesos, but meanwhile they were able to build both a good schoolhouse for themselves and huts in which to live. The women worked the land while their husbands helped with the construction or went off to the coffee plantations to earn the money to pay for their share of the land. They decided to call the place La Independencia. Although it is small and very poor, today it shines with a number of brick houses built by Marcelo's former students who have become teachers themselves. At last count, over twenty of Marcelo's students had become teachers and many more had finished sixth grade too young to teach.

Marcelo had to struggle harder than any of the other teachers to free the baldíos, for few of the owners have given up their workers and their lands happily. Although not all land distribution has been fraught with as much danger, it has often encountered barriers.

The Revolution of 1910 marked a change in the social structure of the Highlands. Many members of the ladino oligarchy, as their lands were distributed, left for Mexico City, making room for a new merchant class to assume positions of leadership in San Cristobal (Vogt 1969:25). Both the INI and the coming of the Pan-American Highway in the early 1950s encouraged social and economic changes as the area opened to more contacts with the outside and as Indians regained their lands and personal rights.

Nevertheless, the region continues to be essentially bicultural, with distinct Indian and ladino settlements and a fairly rigid division of labor. Indians work as peasants and a few as unskilled laborers or servants. Only the poorest ladinos work with their "backs," and they are considered to be little "better" than Indians; many of them, indeed, are themselves acculturating Indians or second generation ladinos. It is expected that ladinos fill roles as merchants, artisans, clerks, and professionals, for they form a class that works with it's "heads" and that considers itself vastly superior to the Indians (Colby and van den Berghe 1961).

Most of the Indians are monolingual in one of many dialects of Tzotzil or Tzeltzal with, at best, knowledge of a pidgin Spanish. Ladino merchants, on the other hand, often speak a pidgin Tzeltzal-Tzotzil, but they consider themselves monolingual in Spanish. Many of the elite make serious efforts to learn English and other prominent languages. The world of the Indians centers upon their tribal region, whereas the ladinos face outward toward the Mexican nation and the world.

Other differences concern religious and social custom. The ladinos are avowed Roman Catholics; the Indians' religion, however, combines many elements of pre-Columbian belief and ritual with some elements of Roman Catholicism. The Indians of some municipios may turn to ladinos as godparents for their children, but the reverse is rarely true. Ladinos are expected to register their marriages with the civil authorities, followed by a church wedding, although the poorest often marry by common law. For most Indians, however, the elaborate and costly pre-Columbian rites suffice, with no attempt at church or civil marriage. One researcher sums up the situation in this way:

> Ladinos generally treat Indians with the condescending kindness accorded a backward child, and the Indians, though latently ambivalent and often hostile to Ladinos, outwardly accept their subservient status. Rigid rules of etiquette help to maintain a social distance, but formal segregation is minimal. Contacts are frequent, especially in the economic sphere, but seldom equalitarian (Vogt 1969:31).

Ladinos were once far more hostile in their treatment of Indians and the latter far more acquiescent than they are now. A common occurrence was for *atajadoras* (literally, grabbers) to wait along the roads leading to San Cristobal as the Indians approached with goods to sell at market. The atajadoras would seize their bundles, throwing minimal sums of money at the Indians, who sometimes tried to pull away but never struck back. The atajadoras would then take their accumulated goods to the market to sell at a stiff mark-up. The INI put a stop to this practice, arresting the atajadoras as complaints were lodged. It also encouraged the building of roads throughout the area and the establishment of truck service along them, enabling Indians to bypass the atajadoras. Although much exploitation continues, mestizos have learned to treat Indians more respectfully. In turn, the Indians have become less acquiescent, more demanding of respectful treatment from the formerly awe-inspiring ladinos.

MATERIAL CULTURE OF THE INDIANS

The Indians have been an agricultural people since their arrival in the area, and farming methods remain almost the same as they were in pre-Columbian times.

The digging stick remains the principal agricultural implement although other tools, especially the hoe and the machete, are also used. The principal crop continues to be corn, "the staff of life," which is supplemented by beans, other legumes, squashes, prickly pears, and, to a lesser extent, apples, pears, peaches, and plums. In the lower (warmer) sections, coffee, sugarcane, hot pepper, and tropical fruits are also grown.

Most farming is done on small plots (milpas), on which corn and beans are planted together and other vegetables sowed between the rows. Primitive means are still used to cultivate the land. Slash-and-burn is the principal method used for clearing the land, and the digging stick often proves to be the tool best suited for planting on the steep hillsides where many Indians are forced to "make milpa" because of the chronic shortage of level land. When the milpas are weeded the edible weeds are allowed to flourish and serve as welcome additions to the usually monotonous diet. Many families also have small vegetable gardens, destined primarily for home consumption. Some raise livestock, but on a small scale. Most women keep a few chickens, reserved usually for ritual meals; eggs are sometimes eaten, but often sold, and are one of the few economic resources of the women. Some of the tribes raise sheep, and for some of them it is taboo to use the sheep for anything other than their wool. The women of Amatenango and Tenango make pottery, which is distributed far and wide over the area. The Chamulas are known for their sale of vegetables, flowers, crude furniture, and home-brewed rum. The Zinacantecos are known for their sale of corn, flowers, and salt; at one time they had a virtual monopoly over salt, but some is now imported from central Mexico.

Although subsistence agriculture is the primary occupation of the Indians, it is often not sufficient to maintain life. Moreover, the people have come to depend upon San Cristobal for some manufactured goods, such as machetes, hoes, and muslin, and for occasional dietary supplements. To obtain money some agricultural products, such as pottery or wool, are sold, and many men and boys do local day labor or go to lowland farms or coffee plantations (fincas) for cash earnings. Since the founding of a coffee workers' union (after the INI's arrival in 1952), working and living conditions on the fincas have improved markedly, and the workers are now sure of receiving their wages. On the fincas, where wages are highest, an average day's labor buys about 15 yards of unbleached muslin or a man's hat. It takes about half a week to earn a good machete.

The most common form of transport within the area is by foot. Some Indians own draft animals, but they are a luxury and slower on the steep trails than are men. Some all-weather roads have been built in the past few years and more are under construction. Passenger trucks, charging a fare equal to about a local day's wages, are becoming more frequent but so far serve only a small portion of the Indian population; most people continue to hike a day or two to reach San Cristobal.

Money occupies a secondary role in the Indian culture; it does not secure status directly for the owner although it is needed to sustain the religious-political roles which do bring status. It is the hard worker who is respected, the lazy one abhorred. There is some division of labor, with men's work centered on farming and women's in the home. The family is seen as an economic unit with each member contributing as he can. Although the women may trail behind their men in public and appear to do some of the heavier tasks such as carrying wood and water, there appears to be a basic equality of the sexes. Public life, especially government and religion, is primarily the sphere of the men, but no major decisions are made without consulting women in the privacy of the home. Women, quite literally, hold the purse strings, for they are entrusted with the care of the family's money. They are also held in some awe for their child-bearing capacities and are often expected to be the sexual aggressors. It is felt by some anthropologists working in the region that they are more conservative than men, more resistant to acculturation.

The people generally live in huts of wattle and thatch, although adobe and brick are coming into more common use, especially near the roads. Where accessible, tile is now preferred to thatch for roofing. The homes are scattered among the corn fields or clustered near one another in *parajes* (hamlets). In the colder regions families tend to live and cook in one-room huts; in the warmer areas separate kitchens are built. Light enters primarily through the door, for most huts have no windows.

Many compounds consist of one or more huts in a large yard, which may be surrounded by a fence. Within the compound may also be found a small vegetable garden, corral, and, depending on the tribe, possibly a steambath. Inside the hut

On the road past Tzontevitz, Chamula.

Oxchuquera carrying sugarcane to market.

Kancuc market.

Chamula home almost hidden by a cornfield.

the furnishings are relatively sparse and decorations are reserved for the altar, if there is one. Blocks of wood may serve as chairs or there may be several small chairs in the room. A miniature, low table may be used for meals, and boards may be laid out in the evening for beds (some tribes have crudely built, permanent, wooden beds). Water and food are stored in jars, and corn is piled in the corner. Firewood is stacked inside or along the outside wall of the house. Other food, implements, and clothing hang from the rafters by rope lines, or they are stuck in chinks in the mud walls. The fire burns or coals glow day and night; after dark additional light may be supplied by pitch brands. Floors are swept daily or several times a week, but with the ever-present mud and domestic animals they usually appear dirty. On festive occasions they may be covered with pine needles.

Commercially manufactured cloth is finding its way into the Indian wardrobe more and more, although many garments are still homespun and woven. Women's dress has remained much the same as in pre-Columbian times: a wrapped or pleated skirt held in place by a wide sash, a loose embroidered tunic worn either inside or outside the skirt, and a large rectangular shawl used for carrying babies and produce. In some places a cloth is worn on the head to prevent sunburn. Women do not wear shoes. The styles of cut, drapery, and embroidery vary from one tribe to another but are almost uniform within the tribe.

Men's clothing, however, shows greater variety from tribe to tribe. Where more conservative forms of dress are maintained, shorts take the place of trousers; short ponchos cover all, but, as with the women, cut, color, and style of embroidery, especially on the shirt, show the origin of the wearer from a distance. Most men now wear store-bought hats and thick-soled sandals. An ever growing number are changing to ladino clothing, which tends to be less expensive but less durable than the older dress.

Anthropologists have often equated a change in clothing with a change in allegiance (for example, Drucker 1963). However, many Indians challenge this, claiming that by changing their wardrobe they are becoming better and more progressive Indians, not ladinos. In Oxchuc most of the men have adopted ladino clothing but claim to be loyal Indians. It may be that a change in allegiance and an orientation to personal rather than community goals and a world beyond the tribe may come with the next generation, although the leaders of Oxchuc, such as Marcelo Santis Lopez, hotly refute this.

SOCIAL STRUCTURE

Families may be either nuclear or extended. Polygamy is recognized in most tribes, but it is too expensive for most men and forbidden to Protestants. Generally the immediate family is nuclear, although, ideally, young couples live first with the family of the bride and then with the family of the groom for the first few years (and children) of their marriage; youngest sons are expected to remain in the homes of their parents, taking care of them and inheriting the greater portion of their property.

In the broader sense, the family consists of the clan (all of those with the same Indian surname). Marriage is taboo within the clan, outside the tribe, sometimes outside certain geographic divisions within the tribe (*barrios*), or with close blood relatives. In some municipios there are only a few clans, thus considerably limiting marriage choices (and adding to a researcher's problems, for it is not unusual to find several children of the same age with the same first and last names in the same class, or indeed to find brothers with identical names!).

The ideal atmosphere is one of happy, calm cooperation among the various busy members of the economic unit, with much show of respect toward one's elders. It is believed that loud noises attract the attention of the gods and that quarreling can cause sickness. While the casual observer may only see people working quietly, almost silently, in their fields or near their homes, quarrels, wife-beatings, adultery, and the like are not uncommon. The eventual separation of a young couple from the home of the groom's parents is usually blamed on quarrels between the young wife and her mother-in-law, but is usually due to tensions between father and son as the youth begins to assert his independence. Generally, marriages are arranged;

the couple may not meet until the first of the ceremonial exchanges which are the essence of the Mayan wedding rites.

A Chamula described his wedding:

We left in the middle of the night, my parents, the *principal* (elder spokesman and community leader), and some of my little brothers. We took 10 liters of liquor and bread and meat. I carried my axe and lots of money. When we got to my future wife's house we surrounded it. It was very important to have people watching on all sides because if we blocked only the door they could dig a hole in one of the other walls and crawl out. When we were ready it was just beginning to get light. The principal began calling to my future father-in-law.

"Good morning, Uncle."

No answer.

"Good morning. Good morning!" After he had called a lot of times my future father-in-law finally said, "Oh, hell, who is it?"

Preparing dinner, Oxchuc.

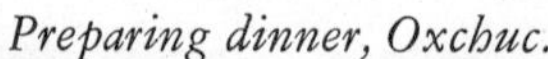

Preparing dinner, Oxchuc.

"Me."

"What do you want?"

"To speak to you."

"What do you want?"

The principal muttered something and then began the ritual chants with which a bride is requested. His first sally was greeted with a loud retort.

"You think I have a daughter? I have no daughters. She's not here. Who sent you? How did you find this house?" He sounded very angry.

But the family was trapped inside. When my future father-in-law finally tired of scolding, he let us in, saying, "You have to see my daughter."

We sat around the fire, toasting one another. I didn't say anything, just served the liquor, but the principal and my parents and my future in-laws kept on talking.

My bride-to-be's father asked when we wanted to take her home with us. I wanted to take her right away. Then the negotiations began. I offered a lot of money, 300 pesos; her father was willing for me to take her that day, but he had to call in all his relatives and his own principales. Everybody had something to drink. There was one man who didn't want things to happen so fast, but we insisted. He gave me lots of advice.

Finally, it was arranged. I only had to stay three days, the day of the wedding, the next day when I chopped wood for my father-in-law all day long, and the final morning when I only did a little work so we could leave early for home. My wife took only a few pieces of clothing, and we agreed to return for a big visit two weeks later. I couldn't do it any other way; I was working in San Cristobal six days a week.

On the next visit we got a lot more advice on how to behave, and again I did some work for my father-in-law.

Marriages in Chamula appear to be worked out more precipitously than in the other municipios once a suitor has been accepted, although this same man had made innumerable visits to the home of another girl only to be rebuffed each time. Unlike courtship patterns in most other tribes, Chamula etiquette requires men to find a bride for themselves even if they only eye her from afar before asking for her hand in marriage. Elsewhere it is usually the boy's mother who searches out the likely prospect and makes the first advances. Once the boy has selected a girl, his family makes several formal visits with gifts of liquor and food, each time judging carefully the extent to which they have been rebuffed, until the girl's family finally weakens and a wedding date is set. The actual wedding is another ceremonial visit, when more and bigger gifts of food and liquor are exchanged, as well as some money, and much advice is given to the young couple on how to conduct themselves as married people. In most municipios the groom then spends a year living with his in-laws, working for them.[3]

RELIGION AND POLITICS

Like so many other aspects of Indian culture, religious beliefs and customs are a blend of Spanish and Mayan, with the latter often predominating. The pre-Columbian legends are retold, sometimes with Catholic or modern elements. A pantheon of deities, many with the names of Christian saints, is worshipped, but each representation of the same saint may possess different powers and be honored accordingly; each wooden cross is also worshipped. Inside the church the people talk to their saints, explaining their troubles and begging for help. They dress the statues in the finest of robes, garland them with necklaces of coins and mirrors, and crown them with wreaths of flowers. The floor is covered with pine needles, and they may burn incense and light candles on the floor as gifts to the saints before they pray. They may also sit about on the church floor, visiting with one another, toasting a saint, drinking in his honor, and nursing their babies. Outside the church they may pray directly to the Sun, the Moon, Mother Earth, the caves and hilltops,

---

[3] For a very detailed description of an elaborate Zinacantecan courtship and wedding see Vogt (1969: 195–217).

and the water holes, each adorned with its cross. Since the end of World War II some Evangelist missionaries associated with the Wycliffe Bible Society have been active in the area and have succeeded in converting about half of the families of Oxchuc, Abasolo, and Tenango. They have met with less success in other tribes.

Ideally, religious and political leadership is shared by all the men of the tribe; status is obtained by fulfilling a succession of religious (and sometimes political) offices. Although the political offices are those required by the Mexican Constitution, the posts carry religious obligations in many of the Indian municipios. The municipal president is often expected to pray for the well-being of his people and to call upon religious precepts as well as "common sense" in his judicial decisions. In several of the municipios Indian teachers have risen in the political hierarchy and now control the presidency; for the most part they ignore the religious obligations of the office or pass them on to others. Some of the presidents, especially the teacher-presidents of Chenalho and Oxchuc, have rejected traditional customs and clothing as they strive to bring their communities more into line with modern Mexican customs.

The only ladino to participate in the tribal government is the Secretary, who is also the only salaried official. In the past, the Secretaries, who are ultimately responsible for all written documents, have used their offices to exploit the Indians. Recently a more honest group has begun to fill the posts and to help the communities.

Life is sacred, for religion and life are one and interwoven. Those who work to preserve life, the *curanderos* (curers, faith healers), are held in much esteem and some awe; Holland (1963) compared them to a priestly class. Healing is accomplished largely through confession and prayer, to the accompaniment of food and drink. Although the use of modern medicine is becoming more popular, especially when the old remedies prove ineffective, the only time that life may be taken, other than the occasional killing of animals for food, is to rid the community of witches. In some tribes it is believed that with increasing age comes increasing knowledge, both good and evil, and that a soul strong enough to absorb so much evil knowledge is strong enough to do harm. The belief in witchcraft serves as a powerful control over individual behavior; those who break with existing customs, amass noticeable wealth, or otherwise endanger the *status quo* are often accused of witchcraft. In times of stress those so accused have been killed. It is my impression that witchcraft may also have been used as a means of ridding communities of nonproductive members, especially the aged and maimed, in times of famine.

Illness is conceived of in spiritual rather than in physical terms, although the symptoms may be palpably physical. Any threat to the harmony which should exist in the world among individuals and in their interactions with the physical and spiritual environment is seen as a grave danger, punished by an attack on the soul. It is through his soul that a man interacts with the mysterious, the supernatural.

> The soul can be lost, captured, or seduced, or one's animal companion may be hidden away or killed. The agent of punishment may be a deity of the earth, the mountains, the water holes, the heavens, one of the Catholic saints in the church, any of the ancestors come to revenge transgressions against the rules related to

Perhaps ladino *medicines are good for something, Chamula.*

them, or living people who, through the strength of their own souls and their communication with the supernatural, can cause trouble and take revenge upon their enemies (Arias Sojob 1970).

The soul may be attacked because of the wrong that one has done, or because it has wandered far away; thus there is considerable danger in traveling far from home.

Illness is conceived of as approaching death, for a part of the soul is dying. Death itself comes with the departure of the entire soul from its rightful place, whether inside one's eyes, in one's head, in a nearby mountain, or in a sacred hilltop or cave. Curanderos are called upon to bring the soul home and return the patient to his rightful place in the community, thus renewing the original harmony in the world, between man and gods, among men, and between man and nature. The curanderos often do succeed in restoring health, especially in the cure of what we would consider psychosomatic illnesses.

The curanderos are thought of as mediators, those who can see beyond the limited vision and understanding of the ordinary human being. The curandero (*jilol*), gifted by his gods, can enter the world of the supernatural and rescue the soul of his patient through his ceremonies and through offerings to those who have hidden the soul and have the power to shorten or prolong its life. The patient who has been cured is restored to the community; the harmony between him and his world is restored (Arias Sojob 1970).

The curing ceremonies vary in detail and elaborateness according to the gravity of the illness, the prescriptions of the curer, and the financial resources of the family. An elaborate ceremony costs several hundred pesos and may leave a family seriously in debt. Such ceremonies can involve the lighting of a large number of candles, diagnosis by means of "pulsing" the patient, confession by the wrongdoer who has brought about the illness through his misconduct, extensive prayers, the eating of a ceremonial meal which includes chicken or some other protein, and considerable drinking. While the illness may be sucked or bled out of the patient, herbs or patent medicines may be administered and steambaths prescribed by those tribes which use them, it is the pulsing and the prayers that form the essence of the ceremony.

A curandero from Chamula describes how he learned to cure and how he practices his art:

God began to teach me to be a doctor when I was about ten. I dreamt that God asked me if I wanted to learn to cure my own children. He said, "Take a little 5-cent candle. Give it to me and I will teach you how to speak to me. First speak to Lord San Salvador, who is in heaven, and then to Lord Saint Vincent, Lord Saint Joseph, Our Lady Saint Mary, Saint John the Baptist (the patron of Chamula), Lord Saint Matthew, Lord Heart of Jesus, Saint Peter, Saint Paul, Lord Just Judge, Lord Saint Anthony, Lord Saint Martin of Porres, Lord Saint Nicholas, Lord Arno, Lord Saint Lorenzo, Lord Ysquipula, and Lord Saint Sebastian. You will talk to all of them." God continued, "Then you will talk to the Virgins: The Virgin of the Rosary, the Virgin Saint Rose, the Virgin of Mercy, the Virgin of Guadalupe, the Virgin of the Assumption, the Virgin of Hope, the Virgin Saint Lucy, the Virgin of Carmen, the Virgin of Candelaria, the Virgin Margarite, and the Sainted Earth." He told me all of that in my first dream.

The second dream came a year later. There were 50- and 20- and 10-cent candles, some of wax and some of parafin; some were green, some red, and some yellow. God told me in which parajes I could cure. My first patient would have to be two years old, the second ten years old, and the third twenty years old.

For the third dream there was a candle of 5 pesos and another of one peso. Again God received the candles and told me how to cure. Two years later there was another dream and God asked me if I still knew what he had taught me. He said, "Let's see. Tell me, as I told you the last time." Well, my soul is clever, so I was able to tell him everything; I had forgotten nothing.

"Well! Now you know with which gods to speak. Never forget what I have told you," he said. Then he told me how much incense I must buy, and laurel, orange twigs, and tender pine branches I must gather.

Five years later I had another dream and again God asked me what I had learned. I had forgotten nothing, not the names of any of the Virgins, nor how many candles, nor that a one-peso tallow candle was needed to bless the Sainted Earth. By the time I was about twenty-two years old He had taught me how to cure. I asked Our Lord Jesus Christ if I could now cure, if I could pulse well. He told me that I could cure anyone who was ill, men or women, boys or girls, and that I could cure them well.

When the daughter of one of my younger sisters took sick she asked me if I would like to cure her. I said I could. I pulsed the baby; she was very sick. I got candles for 50 cents and 20 cents and two for 5 cents, and with those (and the attendant prayers) she got a little better. Then my father took sick and asked me to cure him. I said I could and listened for the sickness in his blood. I got candles for 50 cents and 20 cents and 5 cents, and thirteen tender pine branches, thirteen laurel twigs, and thirteen of orange. With this (and the prayers) he got better. Then my mother took sick, her body ached all over. When I pulsed I found a tumor in her stomach; it was as big as an apple. It was the *poslom* [devil]. I gathered about forty different herbs in the woods; with these my mother got better. Then a sister got sick. I bought a peso's worth of sulphur, a tobacco leaf, a head of garlic, and a little liquor, and she got better. She had eaten a chicken, which made her sick; she had been vomiting. When she ate fish she also vomited. But with this medicine she could eat all the chicken she wanted.

Not all of us doctors use the same treatments. We each do as our God has taught us; every doctor has his own God. Not all the Gods speak in their dreams, like mine. Others go to the Holy Mountains and give their candles, 10- and 5- peso candles and two 5-peso tallow candles; that is how they cure their patients. I don't know how to cure that way, so I don't go to the mountains. I go to the Church of Lord Just Judge and the Church of Lord Saint Anthony and Lord Saint Arno and to the Church of Saint Dominic. When the illness is very grave and I've finished going to all the churches, I return to the house and give more one-peso wax candles, yellow and green, and a wax and a tallow candle worth 50 cents each, pine branches and orange and laurel twigs and incense, and a hen if the patient is a woman, but a rooster if he is a man, and a liter of liquor and four big bottles of Fanta soda. That is how the patient recovers, even if he has been very ill.

Another curer, also a Chamula, reported:

I became a curer because of a sickness I once had. I almost died that time. My father had gotten drunk; we were walking along together. I was playing around, lighting little fires along the edge of the road so that we could see our way. "Hurry up," I said to my father and to his friend who came with us. The owners of the grass came out and raised a rumpus because I was burning their grass. I took fright and became rooted to the spot. The earth imprisoned me. A little while passed and I became gravely ill. After all, we never should play with fire, since it is Our Lord. He became very angry and took his vengeance upon me. Fire burst forth everywhere, from my mouth, my eyes; it was as though I was crazy. Not only had I played with Him; I had urinated on Him, too.

My father found a doctor for me. The doctor said it was insanity and began to cure me with herbs; he stuck them up my nose and I nearly died from those herbs. I wasn't eating any more [a sign of impending death]; they said there was no other cure. For three days I didn't eat because they said I was dying. I couldn't open my eyes any more, I couldn't move, I couldn't even swallow water; the little that I drank they fed me with a leaf.

Then I died. My parents began to mourn for me; the whole family gathered. My pulse was beating very weakly. I had died; for three days and three nights I was unconscious.

I dreamt that they carried me to the graveyard and were digging my grave. I was saved because the tunic on which I was lying slipped. If it hadn't fallen who knows what would have happened to me. They would have buried me. I saw that it was lying at the edge of the grave and that the cross had already been installed.

The cross was like a God. I saw three Lords seated along the path. When they were ready to bury me and had lifted me up to move me over to the grave my tunic fell and someone said to pick it up. Then I heard the song of some birds and the sobbing of some children who had placed themselves at my head to defend me. The children saved me. When I woke up I was in the church and some ladies were holding me up. I [my soul] went to the church after they took me out of the grave and that is where I awoke.

That's how I received the gift of curing. The Gods gave me everything that a curer needs, the gourd cup, the flowers, everything. I still couldn't get them myself, but the people helped me. Then I could walk again, but only with help. After that dream I was able to cure.

Still, practice and ability are different; at first we are afraid and don't know what to say. I didn't have confidence in myself until after my third dream. It is only then that we gain confidence and know what to say. Then we understand that Our Father in The Heavens inspires us every time.

My second and third dreams were like the first, also during times of grave illness. After those dreams I began to cure my own children. I could understand what type of illness a person had, whether it was fear or fever or whatever.

Once the people knew that I was curing my own children they began asking me to cure their relatives. I did a lot of curing, in many places. Once one of my sons was sick and it looked like there was no way of curing him; we had already heated the water with which to bathe him before the burial. Thanks to my ability I was able to save him. That's how I learned to cure.

I was still drinking then. God told me to go forth and help others. When we practice this art we have to drink, but we always find youths or girls who don't want to drink and they ask our help. We get drunk and can't finish the cure, so we return home.

Later the same Lord told me to stop curing, for sometimes I was mistreated because of my drunkenness. So as soon as I found other work I stopped curing. When I cured I used to travel very far, but once the Lord told me to stop, I did. Destiny had chosen me for other things. Since I was able to find other work I am tranquil; God himself has ordered me to do what I am doing now.

Well, sometimes I still do some curing; I haven't forgotten everything yet. But I have stopped drinking. I ask for what is necessary for the cure but I let the people drink by themselves. God advised me that way; after all, what is most important is that the prayers turn out right.

That's how I learned to cure. And that's why it makes me laugh when the *gringos* [North Americans] here tell me they want to learn. I tell them to learn if they can, but I also tell them it's impossible, that it doesn't depend on them but it is a gift given from On High. I have told them a lot about the art of curing and they themselves say they can't learn on their own.

If we practice without permission the illness can turn on us, and we can become sick with it. There was one friend [an anthropologist] here who wanted to learn; I told him he couldn't but he said he could. He would kneel with us when we prayed, and listen, and write. But he didn't learn. We cure one way, the ladino doctors another.

The schools have made some attempt to introduce the germ theory of disease, but with relatively little success except, perhaps, in half-Protestant Oxchuc. There, and to a lesser extent in other municipios, injections and aspirins have replaced or supplement the curing ceremonies. These medicines are obtained through a variety of sources. Sometimes they are bought from local ladinos or in the pharmacies of San Cristobal; more often they are purchased at dispensaries supported by various governmental and religious organizations, including the Secretariat of Health, the National Indian Institute (INI), the Evangelist Church, the Marist Brothers, and the Jesuits, among others. Some dispensaries are better stocked than others, although the government agencies appear to operate on the lowest budgets.

These dispensaries (*clínicas*) are generally staffed by Indian nurses (medical assistants), men who have been trained to make simple medical diagnoses along western precepts, administer the more common medicines, and do minor surgery.

Physicians visit periodically. Whenever they can, the people shop around for the best available cure.

With the preferred recourse to curanderos rather than to medical doctors, no statistics are available regarding physical or emotional health. Tropical diseases are rare in the Highlands and resistance to subcutaneous infection appears to be much greater than among ourselves; intestinal and pulmonary diseases appear to be the principal causes of mortality among both adults and children. While water is plentiful, much of it is found in stagnant water holes. Some teachers make half-hearted attempts to teach the people to boil their drinking water but they are rarely successful. Although houses almost universally lack windows, the many spaces left for the escape of the smoke from the open hearth make them quite drafty. Tuberculosis is also common and the bacilli find a welcome haven in the damp, dark huts. The principal item of diet is corn, which has been soaked in lime and which is taken in some form at every meal. It can be the only course, but it is generally supplemented by chili, a fine source of vitamins, beans, a green vegetable, and occasionally coffee, eggs, fruit, berries, meat, or chicken. The intake or protein is limited, with meat or chicken generally restricted to ceremonial occasions. People tend to be short of stature, perhaps averaging slightly under five feet.

THE LADINOS

The ladino economy is far more diversified than that of the Indians. Although agriculture is the backbone, major sources of income include commerce, the manipulation of real estate, construction, some small-scale manufacturing, and positions within the Mexican bureaucracy. There are also a number of doctors and dentists in San Cristobal, and many lawyers, since the State University School of Law is located there. Agriculture continues to depend heavily on human labor rather than on machinery. Commerce and trade operate on all levels, from petty shopkeepers with minimal wares displayed at the entrance of their houses; to small-scale artisans, such as leather workers, candlemakers, and blacksmiths, who sell their wares locally; to small wholesalers and middlemen who supply the several hundred stores in the area; to small manufacturers who export their wares nationally and even internationally. Trucking is limited to the few roads, but mule trains crisscross the trails of the back country, buying primarily coffee and selling a variety of small goods at the weekly markets in many of the more remote municipios.

Atajadoras no longer enjoy the steep markups they once knew when they seized Indians' goods at the edges of San Cristobal, and the general standard of living in the area appears to have risen in the past few years. The Indians now have more money to spend in the many little shops that line the principal business streets and which cater almost exclusively to them.

Standards of living vary widely among the ladinos of San Cristobal. At the top are the remnants of the old oligarchy and those newly arrived to positions of leadership, most of whom are considered quite wealthy by general Mexican standards. At the bottom are the poorest of the newly ladinized, who know hunger, inadequate shelter, ragged clothing, and cold. Most of the people range between the two extremes, although only the richest appear to enjoy truly adequate diets, clothing, or shelter.

Many of the houses of San Cristobal look quite old; some were built during the sixteenth and seventeeth centuries, but newer ones are built so much like their predecessors that, with the rapid formation of mold on stucco and brick, the town appears to have just awakened from the colonial period. The homes of the wealthy are generally built in traditional hacienda style with the better rooms opening onto long porches surrounding a patio garden and with the workrooms facing out to the back and an open work area. The poorest people construct windowless wattle or plank huts roofed with tar paper, poor even by Indian standards. Their huts usually stand in a small work yard which gets quite muddy in the rains. Others rent small rooms in larger houses, rooms which are often bereft of water or any sanitary facilities.

The homes of the wealthiest are furnished with antiques, expensive factory-made items shipped in from central Mexico, the United States, and Europe, or with local hardwood imitations of them. The poorest ladinos tend to furnish their homes much as do the Indians, although they strive to use ladino furnishings as much as possible. Prominent in almost every home, regardless of economic level, is the altar, decorated with pictures and a small statue or two of the saints, flowers, glasses with candles in them, and, in the lower-class homes, important objects unrelated to religious service, such as a pencil and a small notebook. The wealthier homes have a bedroom for every two or three members of the family and quarters in the back for the servants; they also have a receiving room, a large parlor, a dining room, and storage space in the back. The poorest have only one room in which they sleep, cook, eat, and store their belongings. Most homes have no provision for heating, although warmth is supplied from the cooking fires of the poorest; some of the wealthiest now have fireplaces. When the weather turns particularly cold and damp many people can be seen huddled around small charcoal braziers.

There is also a miniature but growing colony of foreigners in the town, most of them from North America. They are considered to be among the wealthiest people, although they usually dispute this heartily. Their homes are either typical of the upper class ladinos or have a combination of North American and local features, but all decorate with many more local artifacts and weavings than do the wealthy ladinos.

The ladinos strive to dress in the latest European and North American fashions; the wealthiest achieve this easily, but the poorest often wear ragged and ill-fitting clothing. There is a bevy of tailors and dressmakers active in the town, for almost all clothing is made to order. Ladinos almost always spurn Indian clothing, although some do wear the heaviest woolen Chamula or Zinacantecan men's outer garments on the coldest days.

As may be gathered from the above, there are a number of clearly recognized social classes in San Cristobal. This contrasts sharply with the Indian communities, where social classes are rarely recognized. At the top of the pyramid are the ladino remnants of the old oligarchy, the newly wealthy, especially a number of merchant families, and most of the foreigners. Below come the small shopkeepers and artisans, who can look down upon the poorest ladinos who must do manual labor and work as servants. But even the poorest can still look down on the Indians. All classes tend to socialize only among themselves, although formal family celebrations often find members of the lower classes present as the poor come to honor their patrons.

Families may be nuclear or extended at all social levels, although the nuclear family is generally preferred. Polygamy is unrecognized, but, as in all places where *machismo* (highly ritualized displays of masculinity) abounds, adultery is common, especially among the men, and the institution of the *casa chica* (mistress's house) is well recognized. Wives are expected to remain faithful to their husbands and to uncomplainingly suffer their peccadilloes in silence. Most people seek their marriage partners from within their own social class, but men seek their mistresses from below.

Most girls marry in their late teens, but men may remain single until their forties; most, especially those of the lower classes, marry during their late teens or early twenties. Following a long and carefully chaperoned engagement, the marriage ceremony is made as elaborate as possible, with extravagant fiestas for both the civil and church weddings. In preparation for the church service the bride is dressed in a long white gown with flowing veil (copied out of the latest French edition of Vogue Magazine), and the streets between the cathedral and the place of the reception are strewn with pine needles. After the church wedding and party are over, the couple is expected to go off on a honeymoon. The lower classes can ill afford this type of wedding, much as they may wish it, and common-law unions are the rule.

Children are desired and are expected to bind the marriage and new home together; they are usually named after the saint of their birth date; saints' days rather than birthdays are celebrated. As in much of the rest of the country, the first child is expected to be born more than nine months but less than a year and a quarter after the wedding; birth control is frowned upon, although the newly rich, with their aspirations for supplying university-level education for all their sons, often have fewer children than the poorest.

The ladinos look outward toward the world; their loyalties are national almost as much as local, in contrast to the Indians, who know only tribal loyalties. Ladinos are, almost without exception, avowed Roman Catholics and strongly censure lack of church attendance. They claim to maintain no vestiges of Indian beliefs, but, at least among the lower classes, several common rites and beliefs persist. For example, both Indians and lower-class ladinos serve a tortilla with a hole in the middle to toddlers, "so that they will talk well." Lower-class ladinos also beg the services of curanderos, sometimes in preference to store-bought medicine. Many curanderos of renown live along the edges of the town among the newly ladinized. Although accurate health statistics are no more available for the ladinos than for the Indians, health and longevity appear to reflect social class, the wealthiest eating well and using medical specialists in Tuxtla, the state capital, or in Mexico City to treat their more serious illnesses. The poor ladinos eat inadequately, use cheap patent medicines or home remedies, and probably have about the same mortality rates as the Indians.

Politics and religion are sharply divided in San Cristobal, at least on the surface.

As in the Indian communities, municipal authorities follow the dictates of the Mexican Constitution, but here they more closely resemble the ideals of that document. San Cristobal is the seat of the state and federal district courts, of the INI center, of fourteen zones of school inspection covering at least twenty-six municipios,[4] and of many other state and federal offices. The town presidency and other elective offices are often looked upon as undesirable in themselves but as necessary stepping stones to major elective posts such as that of State Governor or Representative to the National Chamber of Deputies.

Clerical functions are performed by the Roman Catholic clergy at a multitude of churches and other church-related institutions; the city of San Cristobal is the seat of the Bishop of Chiapas. The ladinos consider themselves to be very religious and virtually ostracize the handful who do not attend mass faithfully every Sunday. Indeed, regular church attendance is often deemed more important than any peccadilloes a man may commit outside the church.

If, in their religious activities, the ladinos appear much the same as they have over the centuries, in other respects they are changing rapidly. Whereas before the construction of the roads it took days to reach Mexico City, it is now possible to be there in four or five hours by a combination of automobile and airplane. San Cristobal has electricity, telephones, telegraph, piped drinking water, and is expanding its sewage system. The clothing styles of Mexico City, North America, and Europe are copied as much as possible. National magazines and the newspapers of Mexico City circulate at least among the upper classes. The wealthier send their children off to study at the National University in Mexico City and the youngsters return trying to change the customs of their elders. Tourists, too, leave behind notions of the world outside. The ladinos look to that world for leadership; they want to join it.

---

[4] As of 1972. The inspection zones were reallocated for the 1972–1973 academic year and new centers established for some of them in Bochil and Ocosingo.

2 / Early childhood

Although some aspects of children's lives vary from one tribe to another, the differences are minor compared to the general patterns common to all. Childhood begins with birth and ends when adolescents become parents themselves. There is little clear age grading; indeed, few people know their exact ages, although birth order is important and remembered. The terms that cover the different stages of childhood are used flexibly according to the nuances or etiquette of a given situation. Although many other terms exist, newborns are most often called *nene* among the Tzotzil and *alal* among the Tzeltal; other Tzotzil terms, especially *olol* or *unen*, are sometimes used to describe toddlers. At about the age of three the generic terms for boy (*kerem*) and girl (*tseb*, Tzotzil; *achix*, Tzeltal) come into use, along with modifiers to indicate the child's level of maturity. Thus, in Oxchuc the young boy or girl who does little more than play and fetch an occasional item for his mother is called *ch'in kerem* or *ch'in achix*, *ch'in* meaning little; the corresponding Tzotzil terms are *bik'it kerem* and *bik'it tseb*. Sometimes *k'osh*, implying the spoiled, youngest child, is used instead of ch'in or bik'it. The child who begins to do chores at about the age of six or seven is known simply as kerem or achix (tseb in Tzotzil).

BIRTH AND NEONATAL STAGE

Sterility is recognized in both men and women, although more commonly blamed on the women. Local herbs or medicines bought in the pharmacies of San Cristobal may be used to insure fertility. Herbs are also taken by some women for birth control or to induce abortion, apparently to no avail, but western medicine or surgical procedures are almost universally unknown. Unmarried mothers, however, are sometimes suspected of committing infanticide.

The man's role in procreation is known, but it is often assumed that he must have sexual relations with his wife every night for a month in order for her to become pregnant. The woman knows herself to be pregnant after missing one or two periods (moons), after which she informs her husband, mother, and mother-in-law. She is expected to suffer nausea during the early stages of pregnancy and to have strong food whims.

Some informants attach little importance to these whims, feeling that no serious ills will result if frustrated, but others describe considerable efforts by husbands or by the expectant mothers themselves to satisfy the whims, which could be for a particular food, especially a seasonal fruit, or which might be to eat the food prepared for another family. Serious consequences are often attributed to the poor nourishment and consequently weakened condition of the mother if her food whims are frustrated; these include miscarriages, premature or still births, weak and sickly newborns, or the death of the parturient mother.

Both parents and grandparents are expected to be happy upon knowing that there will be a birth in the family; jealousy is sometimes expected in the siblings. Women themselves, however, appear to be less than overjoyed at having many children. A woman from Chenalho said, "After six children you get very tired and weak. After eight you don't want any more, but you have to bear up." A young Oxchuquera, the oldest of her three children barely four years old and her fourth soon to be born, said, "You get tired of having children. But what can you do as long as you're with your husband?" While some deny that they expect any of their children to die, the realities of a high child-mortality rate demand large families so that some of the children may survive into adulthood.

There is some preference for boys, especially by the men, but ideally the family has both boys and girls, providing each of the parents with his helpers. Nothing is done to determine the sex of the child, although prayers are sometimes offered to some of the saints when there is a strong sex preference. This is most likely to happen after there have been several children of one sex and none of the other. Boys are generally preferred for the first birth to insure an heir for the family's land.

Women are held to be more responsible for their children's welfare than men and are more apt to be blamed for the death of a child. However, misconduct on the part of either parent may endanger a child's health, either directly (for example, a drunken father who exposes his baby to the night air when returning home, thus leading to pneumonia, or a mother who carelessly allows her children to eat diarrhea-causing foods or to catch colds which develop into pneumonia) or in-directly (by exposing the child to soul-loss).

Twins appear to be viewed idiosyncratically. Some informants feel that they come from eating certain foods, such as bananas or prickly pears, and relate the multiple births to the many seeds in these fruits or to eating twinned fruits. One woman felt that Jesus Christ wanted the mother to bear twins.[1] Most informants, however, can give no explanation for multiple births. Some women consider twins an unexpected blessing, since an additional child is added to the family, but many are more concerned with the extra burdens of nursing and rearing two children and with the high probability that the babies will die within the first few months of life.

Witchcraft is often called upon to explain malformed children, or it is believed that the moon (*Ch'ulme'tik*, Mother of the Sun) was angered when she saw the

---

[1] Ambivalent feelings are expressed about Christ. On the one hand He is known as the Son of God and identified with the Sun God, a principle deity who Himself was known to have been a very naughty little boy before ascending to the heavens to illuminate the earth. Christ is also known, at least in some tribes, to be weak and no friend of man in His present imperfect state.

parents quarreling. Since it is assumed that spouses will disagree, pregnant Oxchuqueras are warned not to look at the moon unless they have taken the precaution of wearing a red ribbon in their belts so that the moon may eat it and leave the baby alone. If other birth mishaps, such as still births, difficult labor, prematurity, or the death of the mother, are not attributed to the frustration of the mother's food whims, they may be blamed on witchcraft or on physical or character weaknesses in the parents. Natural abortions are sometimes attributed to the workings of the devil in his personification as a monkey (*max*). It is said that the max steals the fetus from one woman to implant it in another's womb, where it may remain for only about five months to be born abnormally small and then to die. The death of the mother or the infant may also be blamed on an inefficient or careless midwife. Some women feel that natural abortions or premature labor result from carrying very heavy objects, yet most women continue hauling water and wood until the last days of pregnancy.

There are no food prohibitions during pregnancy, and women are expected to perform all their tasks as long as they possibly can, even through the early stages of labor. It is only after the pains become very strong that a woman informs her husband, who should remain close at hand during the last days of the pregnancy. He is likely to advise an older woman, often his mother or mother-in-law, who then acts as midwife and whom he assists. In Chamula, women tend to call on neighbor midwives who may not be relatives.

The birth almost always takes place inside the home. During the day the children are sent out to play but are not otherwise excluded. Indeed, by the time a girl is ready to have her first child it is expected that she has seen several births; the same holds true for her young husband. In Amatenango, however, only the older adults attend the birth; a young husband is excluded along with his younger siblings.

The woman crouches on the floor, fully clothed but with her sash loosened, supported by her husband or his surrogate. He or the midwife massages and presses on her abdomen, and receives the child as it falls onto a little pile of soft rags, leaves, or an old, straw mat (*petate*). Girls are supposed to fall onto their backs and boys onto their stomachs. If a boy is left lying face up he is likely to turn into a girl, so the person who receives the child immediately checks its sex and makes sure it is left in the correct position.

After the birth the umbilicus is bound, cut with a knife or machete, and the end seared with embers from the cooking fire. In Chenalho a boy's umbilicus is cut over a corncob, a girl's over a grinding stone. The placenta is either thrown away (for the dogs to eat) or buried. In Chenalho, it is felt that if the placenta is buried near the hearth the child will be particularly sensitive to cold and suffer from consequent stomachaches; he will be less sensitive if it is buried near the door, and least so if it is buried outside. In Oxchuc it is often buried in a corn field. Other groups seem less concerned with the fate of the placenta, but few are careless with the navel cord which drops from the child after a few days. Almost all fathers take care to hang it high in a tree so that the child will not be afraid to climb. Girls climb less than boys so less care is taken with the disposition of their cords.

After the cord is tied and cut the baby is bathed in warm water to which herbs may be added. In Oxchuc this is done in the steambath (*pus*), when the mother bathes almost immediately after the birth, but elsewhere women wait one to three days before bathing. In Chenalho, where there are no steambaths, some women are reputed to never bathe; instead they may rest on a bed where a space has been left between the planks so that the placenta falls to the floor (to be licked up by the

If the navel cord is hung high in a tree, the children will not be afraid to climb, Chamula.

omnipresent dogs). But other women in Chenalho may go to a nearby stream within a few days of the birth to bathe themselves.

Thereafter the babies are sponged off with tepid water from time to time, but real bathing is considered to take place only in the steambath. Most women bathe themselves and their newborn two or three times a week, but as the baby grows the bathing becomes less frequent. In Amatenango, which does have steambaths, and in Chenalho, where there are none, children are seldom bathed, but elsewhere women tend to bathe their young children whenever they themselves use the steambath.

Once bathed the newborn is dressed in a shirt that may be store-bought flannel or home-woven cotton, bound into a rag or specially woven skirt, and swaddled in several other cloths. Finally, he is wrapped in a blanket, all but hidden from view, and he and his mother are put to rest on a bed. In Amatenango and Chenalho, however, women begin making the baby's first shirt only after his birth, so the baby is merely swaddled for the first two or three weeks of life. Wet skirts are put in the sun or near the fire to dry, but those stained with feces are first scraped or washed. No form of talcum is used.

Grandparents and other very close relatives who have not been present at the birth are informed, but no other announcement is made. News of the birth spreads slowly through gossip.

Some women resume their household tasks within a few days, as soon as they feel able, but others, with parents or in-laws willing to do their work, may be allowed to rest as long as twenty days.

Some families celebrate the birth with a festive meal, consisting primarily of boiled chicken and its broth, and by drinking. In Chenalho a hen is eaten for the birth of a girl, a rooster for a boy. Bread, coffee, or liquor may also be taken or may be substituted for the chicken. Some, however, do not celebrate the birth in any way. A midwife may be paid, in addition to the meal, 5 pesos or forty ears of corn for the birth of a girl, 10 pesos or sixty ears of corn for a boy; this is especially likely where the midwife has performed in an official capacity rather than merely as an older relative of the mother. In Amatenango, where women are often economically independent, the midwife receives the same fee, generally 10 pesos, regardless of the sex of the child.

The newborn is put to the breast as soon as he begins to whimper; it is believed that the sucking will stimulate the flow of the milk, and that if he is not put to the breast immediately he will die. Mothers with insufficient milk are first fed sweetened rice and then a special, spiced corn gruel or herb tea to stimulate the flow. When this does not suffice a wet nurse may be sought temporarily; if there is sufficient money powdered milk and bottles are used, although this is felt to be a poor substitute for the mother's own milk, without which the baby cannot thrive. Poorer people feed their newborns cooked corn gruel (*atole*) when the mother cannot nurse; such babies rarely survive.

The baby is carefully hidden from the view of all but the immediate family to guard against soul-loss, especially during the first twenty days of life. Thereafter, he is watched carefully; falls are particularly dangerous since the soul, which is only tenuously attached to the newborn, is likely to become detached from a fall. Women often sleep apart from their husbands during those first twenty days.

INFANCY

In Oxchuc men make a special, small, and rather coarse rope hammock which is padded with one or two blankets and in which the baby is put to sleep during the day; one hammock usually lasts for several children. However, there are times during the day when the baby sleeps on his mother's back, especially if she is busy and there is nobody at hand to help swing his hammock. Tzotzil women almost always sleep their babies on their backs throughout the day. The swaddling helps hold the baby securely on his mother's back. At night babies sleep on the parent's bed, either between the mother and the wall or between the parents. Other children who share the same bed may not be allowed to sleep next to the newborn for fear that they will crush him. Lullabies are unknown, but women bounce and pat the babies on their backs or swing them in their hammocks, often shushing them ("sh-sh-sh") at the same time.

In Chamula girls' hair is cropped once during the second year of life to stimulate its growth, and boys' hair is also cut then for the first time. Since it is felt that premature haircutting may leave a child mute, the first barbering is usually delayed until he has begun to form words clearly. In most other municipios girls' hair is never cut and boys receive their first barbering, at the hands of their mothers, at about two years of age. Men and boys are supposed to wear their hair short, in very conservative western style, although some wait months between barberings. As soon as girls' hair is long enough, it is braided into two plaits; this is the common style for both girls and women, who often braid ribbons into their hair. Like the rest of their garments, the particular style and color of the ribbon varies from one tribe to another, as does the way in which the braids may be joined. Men wear no adornments in their hair. Either special hats are provided for the babies or their heads are wrapped in a shawl or a piece of the baby sling. In those communities where women use earrings the ears may be pierced after about three weeks or the piercing may be delayed for months or even years; a red-hot needle is used and some thread is left in the lobes. However, many women, especially Tzotzil, do not use earrings. No other piercing or shaping is done, nor is there any circumcision. Many babies have small pieces of amber (called The Tears of St. Peter; now generally plastic substitutes) tied to their wrists to keep away the evil eye, and small gourds to distract, entertain, and encourage them to move their hands. In Zinacantan they also wear a small bag with bits of camphor, garlic, and thyme inside.

Nursing is always on demand, and babies are rarely allowed to whimper for more than a few moments before being put to the breast. When women can, they sit cradling their children in their arms, especially during the first few months, but often, and especially when away from home, they do not interrupt their other activities to feed their children. Rather, a mother is likely to move her baby, sling and all, so that instead of resting on her back he hangs in front of her; then, as she proceeds with whatever she has been doing, she offers him the breast. It is not unusual to see a Chamula woman, a load of wood on her back, a toddler perched on top, and a smaller infant hanging in front, trudging up one of the steep mountain trails. Others, however, endeavor to leave at least one of the babies at home if going nearby for water or wood.

Sometimes during the second half of the first year the milk begins to be supplemented, first by atole and by the liquid in which beans have been cooked. When children start to reach for them, at about one year of age, they are given tortillas and uncooked corn gruel. Some mothers prechew the tortillas, but others feel that children will not fatten or that they will become stupid if they do not chew their own food. To encourage their children to chew for themselves, Amatenangueras are likely to blow onto their baby's mouths. As a child learns to eat them, other foods are introduced until, sometime during the second or third year of life, he eats the basic adult diet and begins to eat chili. In Chamula and sometimes in Zinacantan, liquor is also introduced as soon as children are able to drink from a glass. At first sparing amounts are given during ceremonial occasions, but the child is included in the family round of drinking. The amounts are gradually increased and it is not unusual to see, during some of the major fiestas, drunken Chamula boys of about ten, although most still drink sparingly at this age and well into adolescence. Women and girls are expected to drink less, although occasionally older women do get drunk. In most other tribes youngsters do not begin to drink liquor until their teens, although it may have been served medicinally since infancy.

Babies are seldom weaned before the advanced stages of the mother's next pregnancy or, if there is no other child forthcoming, until the age of three or four. Some women, however, do not wean their lap babies even during the last stages of pregnancy and others have been known to nurse until the child is over six. Once weaned, most children will drink no more milk for the rest of their lives. Weaning is accomplished rapidly, generally in less than a week, and with little fuss. At night the mother turns from her baby and the father may embrace and cuddle him; during the day she either denies him her breast or smears it with chili or some unpleasant tasting herb. Also, he may be offered food every time he cries for the breast. Once weaned, the child is no longer allowed to sleep with his mother.

The child's first cry is taken as a sign of life. After that, crying is generally attributed to hunger, pain, fright, anger, or, for older children, sorrow. Upon whimpering the breast is offered. When this does not quiet him, the baby's other needs are immediately looked into. A mother will often neglect her other work in order to comfort her infant; when other provisions fail, as they often do with colicky babies, she will say special prayers, at home and in church, to help quiet him. Only a very few think to use medicines to calm their children, but some do consult curers and perhaps hold curing ceremonies.

Children are expected to be able to open their eyes at birth, but not to recognize anything or anyone. At about the age of three weeks they should respond to noises, especially those made to awaken them. At two months they are expected to begin to distinguish sounds. By three months of age they should recognize their mothers and a month later begin to smile, especially in response to tickling. By five months they should begin to babble and, a month later, to reach for objects, holding the smaller ones, such as a piece of banana, a tortilla, or a little gourd cup; they should also attempt to chew despite an insufficient number of teeth needed to masticate adult food effectively. By this age parents have begun to nuzzle, kiss, or suck on the baby's nose, chin, cheek, or ears, sometimes whispering that they would like to eat him. It is only with babies that they express tenderness physically, at least in front of others; later almost all affection is expressed verbally.

By the age of one year a child is expected to recognize people, distinguish tastes, be able to see about forty meters, and be on the verge of speaking clearly, having begun to babble months earlier. By the age of two his sense of hearing should be fully developed; by the end of the next year his sense of smell should have become fully developed. Yet one mother said, after reaffirming all of the above, "A three-year-old doesn't know anything because he only likes to play." Within the next year the child should learn to dress himself, no longer calling for all of his clothing to be warmed over the fire before being put on him. By five his sense of sight should be fully developed, so that he can see as far as an adult; there is little concern with the fine eye-muscle control needed for reading in these still largely nonliterate societies. Girls, whose weaving and embroidery require eye-muscle control which may be similar to that needed for reading, do not begin to undertake those skills until several years later.

EARLY EDUCATION

Parents are very permissive with their babies, making no demands upon them but rather following their leads. There is no pressure to show signs of precocity, yet parents delight in each new development. They cuddle, kiss, and talk to their babies frequently. There is some baby talk but most parent–child conversation is rather adult in tone if simple in content. Adult rhetoric requires that a listener participate actively in a narration by echoing the speaker's last word or phrase after almost every sentence. Parents feel duty-bound to respond to all their child's utterances, both to encourage the development of speech and to prevent soul-loss. When awake a child is often bound on his mother's back, his head at her shoulder so she has merely to turn her head as she works for their eyes to be at almost the same level and for adult-like conversations to take place.

In order to speed up a child's acquisition of speech a toddler is given a tortilla which has been made with a hole in the middle. In Oxchuc one such tortilla is eaten by the child in each of the corners of the house for four successive meals. Bananas are also considered helpful for preventing mutism.

A baby spends most of his day on his mother's back, especially when she has work to do. He is only put to sleep in a hammock or on a bed if there is someone close at hand to watch him or if her work is not so pressing that she cannot take time out to attend him. However, children's motor development does not appear to be much retarded by this confinement. In many respects they appear to develop about a month later than our babies, but how much this is due to physical restric-

Chamula woman spinning, her child on her back.

tions and how much to genetic or dietary differences is not possible to determine at this time (Robey 1969).

When not tied to the mother's back babies spend most of their waking hours in the arms of an older relative. They are given objects to grasp, especially soft, leafy branches, which they are encouraged to wave and bounce. They are allowed to crawl on the bed when someone is able to attend them, or on a petate; however, crawling on the ground or on the dirt floor of the house is discouraged. They are encouraged to stand, first with help and then alone, and to walk. Parents pull a baby along with them in an effort to teach him to walk. However, some do not consider children able to walk until they can manage the slippery trails near their homes. Crawling and teething tend to occur at about the same time, and some parents feel that children vomit when they start to crawl. This is believed due to some fault, hostility, or ill-behavior on the part of one or both of the parents, and the condition is cured by a prayer ceremony for the entire family. The ceremony involves confessions of sins before the entire family and a steambath for both the sinner and the child. Others attribute the illnesses that accompany crawling to the coldness of the ground or to the fact that the baby is likely to play with and eat dirt. Some

Chamula weaver.

children are known to walk before a year, most at about a year and a half, but some are not considered able to walk until close to three years of age. This late development is considered due to weakness, especially because of poor diet, or because the child is lazy, naughty, or willful.

At the same time that they are encouraged to walk, children are carefully protected from falling, lest they lose their souls. Big falls are considered very serious crises and may be remembered for life. A Chamula woman reported:

> One time, when I could barely walk, I suddenly slipped and rolled down to the bottom of a ravine. It was very steep and I scratched my stomach. I was badly frightened. My mother asked, "Have you stopped falling?" and I said, "Yes, I've stopped." Then I began to cry. It all happened because I didn't want to stay home. I didn't really know how to walk then but my mother had had another baby and couldn't carry me any more. My mother said to me, "Now you understand why I didn't want to bring you along!" Luckily I only scraped my stomach. About a week later I took sick. My mother said it was because I hadn't wanted to stay home. My parents sought a curer; really I (my soul) had remained there where I had fallen. I was vomiting all the time and had continual diarrhea. They cured my fright; that's how I recovered.

Children appear to learn all other patterns by imitation; these include sitting postures and carrying with the tumpline (a wide band across the forehead from which bundles are carried on the back). They are seldom placed in a sitting or squatting position, in the adult manner, but are rather cuddled or held in the arms; they themselves appear to assume correct positions when they begin to sit unsupported, usually after they have begun to toddle. Mothers may then begin to pull their daughters' skirts down so that their modesty is not threatened, but most girls' skirts are long enough to insure proper covering (for the genitals and thighs). Little concern is expressed for boys' modesty during the early years once they have begun to walk. When toddlers reach for something to carry with a tumpline, often an empty bag or an ear of corn, they are allowed or even helped to sling it from their heads. The tumpline may slip, their heads may wobble, but the usual reaction is to replace the line or to laugh softly as they try to straighten their heads. In this way they learn to carry until girls of three or four are given miniature water jugs to fill when they accompany their mothers for water; boys may then be given a piece of wood to carry home. Although parents urge the child to begin his adult tasks, there is no real insistence on such performance until about the age of six or seven, at which time real, if limited, work is expected of him.

There is no conscious attempt to train children in any way until they give clear evidence of understanding language and have begun to say a few words, often at about the age of one. Women do, however, discourage their babies from biting at their nipples by removing the nipple and by patting the child's mouth with a little scolding, almost as though spanking him, or by pressing his head into the breast or pinching his nostrils closed to momentarily cut off his supply of air. But they claim that children are not teachable at this age, that they never strike their babies, nor make any attempt to teach them not to bite; they say that they must put up with the pain, without recourse, since babies are too young to learn. Neither do they provide any other materials on which teething babies may massage their gums.[2]

Once children are considered teachable, once they have given evidence that they "understand," there is an attempt to teach both proper eating and toilet habits. They are also encouraged to refrain from crying when they fall or hurt themselves. Babies are not allowed to handle or play with corn, although they may be given a fistful to throw to the chickens at feeding time. They are discouraged from wasting or throwing food away, although some parents are stricter than others when it comes to playing with small fruits in season. If food drops on the dirt floor a child may be instructed to feed it to a dog, but more often he is expected to clean off the worst of the dirt and eat it.

Toilet-training is also begun at this time. First a child learns to express his needs. He is taken, and later sent, to a spot just outside the door or to the edge of the patio if he is outside. As his walking improves he is encouraged to move further and further away from the house until he uses the surrounding areas like an adult. At night, however, young children may relieve themselves near an inside wall rather than be sent into the bad night airs; the family dog usually cleans up after them.

Since children often have been displaced by a new baby during the period they are learning to train themselves, it often falls to an older sibling rather than to the mother to teach them. When parents do the training they usually depend upon repeated and very patient instructions in the belief than once the child understands he will conform. Siblings tend to have less patience. To facilitate the training children wear only tunics; boys are not given their first shorts (or trousers) until about the age of six or seven. Girls may continue wearing the infant skirts, especially if woven for that purpose, during the toddler stage, but in most tribes they are dressed in belted, knee-length tunics until they resume wearing skirts at about the age of eight. Children are expected to be reasonably well toilet-trained by the age of four.

Children become ill frequently, and the child mortality rate is quite high, although no reliable statistics are available. In some communities it is estimated that about 20 percent of the children die by the age of four and many older women report having lost more than half of their children. Yet with most women bearing about ten children and with a somewhat lowered infant mortality rate over the past few decades, the Indian population of the Highlands is increasing rapidly, perhaps apace with the rest of the country, which, as of this writing, reports an annual increase of 3 percent, one of the highest in the world!

Childhood illness may be blamed on witchcraft or other causes.

A man from Chenalho recalled:

> I remember being cured one time when I had a tumor on my foot. I was lying in bed, suffering. I'm told that I was very sick, close to death. The curer

---

[2] It is expected that the child begin to replace baby teeth at about six or seven. The mother should throw the lost tooth to the rafters or the roof, asking all the wild animals of the mountains, such as the rat, the frog, or the wild pig, to replace it with a new tooth.

prayed over my foot and the pain lessened. He said I wouldn't die; that made me feel a little better. I was perhaps four or five then. Later, when I was a little bigger they cured my soul. I had a high fever and my body ached. When I was growing up, I suffered a lot from sicknesses. Since we didn't know anything about [modern] medicine then, we suffered more, but when we saw the curer come we felt better. After all, he's a doctor, too, and he tells us whether we're gravely ill or not. When he says we'll get better, once we find the cause of the illness, that it's only temporary, and we'll get well as soon as we know how to cure it, then we are tranquil.

There is some prejudice against left-handedness; it is felt that the right hand is the smarter, especially for fine motor tasks such as sewing. Young children are encouraged to use the right hand and are teased when they do not, but if their preference is strong they are allowed to continue using the left; it is felt that this is their fate.

Verbal skills are generally prized. Children who have trouble learning to speak, even after eating bananas and the special tortillas, are believed to have been hit frequently, especially on the back, or to be the product of an incestuous relationship. The definition of incest varies from one community to another, but parent–child and brother–sister relationships are considered incestuous in all. In many municipios restrictions also apply to the relationships between first cousins, uncle and niece, and aunt and nephew. In many communities kinship is implied among all who have the same Indian surname and in Oxchuc among all with the same Spanish surname in addition. When these clanlike relationships are recognized sexual relations within the group are considered incestuous. Children born of incest or conceived out of wedlock are teased for their ill luck, for, although witchcraft may be blamed for many a misfortune, each person is at the same time considered responsible and blamed for any ills that may befall him or a member of his family. However, these and all other atypical children, including the malformed, are cared for, primarily by the mother. The taking of human life, other than as a defense against witchcraft, is considered the worst of sins; sick and malformed children are cared for either out of a sense of love or of duty, although "damned" children may not be given the same quality of care as healthy ones and occasional infanticide has been rumored. The physically malformed are, at least in part, blamed and teased for their afflictions when they grow older; few appear to survive into adulthood.

The parents of illegitimate or malformed children also become the butt of gossip and teasing. If a woman is unmarried at the time of conception her family usually tries to force a marriage with the baby's father. This happens most often in the case of previously unmarried adolescents, and such a union is considered cheap and unprestigious. Where adultery has been committed the baby's father may be pressured into paying at least a nominal sum toward its upkeep. Since herb-induced abortions are not effective and surgical abortions not practiced, women must keep their illegitimate children or kill them.

Polygamy is not unknown in many municipios although few men practice it; in many cases the second wife is the younger sister of the first. Such marriages may come about when the older woman is ill and unable to fulfill her domestic duties; her younger sister is brought in as a helper. Or, if the second wife is not related to the first, she may be established in a separate and independent house of her own.

A man is considered rich if he can maintain two households, even though the wives and their children may contribute considerably with their labor. Another means of securing extra household help is to "borrow" a younger sister or brother of either of the spouses, or some other closely related child; only on rare occasions is a non-relative brought in. Adoption, as such, is virtually unknown, but young children who have been orphaned of their mother are raised by a closely related woman, preferably a grandmother. An effort is made to place nursing children, including newborns, with a woman who is herself nursing. However, such children are seldom given the same attention as the biological offspring of the family. Occasionally very poor Indians give or sell their children as servants to ladinos.

In many of the Indian communities children born on Sundays are named for that day, others are named according to the next recognized saint to have his fiesta celebrated, and one child is usually named after each of the parents. Each child also carries the Spanish and Indian surnames of the father. On occasion the child may be given all the three names of a beloved relative even if the two surnames differ from his father's. Other parents select the first name by whim, but make their choice from the very limited number of names common within the tribe. In Zinacantan only twenty-seven names are common among the men and sixteen among the women (Vogt 1969:144). In Oxchuc, having selected a name, the parents should inform the person for whom the child is named, usually a close relative or friend. However, they need not ask permission for the use of the name. In recent years Protestant Oxchuqueros have begun to take Biblical names whether or not they have been used in the tribe before, while Catholics refer more and more to the Roman Saints' calendar. In Chamula and Chenalho a child is often given both a name for daily use and a secret real name; often he will not know the latter until he hears his parents tell it to a curer during a healing ceremony. By keeping the real names well hidden parents help protect their children's souls against witchcraft.

Most children are named at about two or three months of age, at which time they are baptized. The baptism takes place in a church and is conducted by a priest. Most people use their tribal church, but some, especially the Chamulas who live near San Cristobal, prefer the more prestigious ladino churches.

Children may be called by their real names in school and when they begin working for ladinos, but within the family and in the local community nicknames are used more frequently. In Chamula, however, the recognized name, in its Tzotzil form, is more commonly used than the nickname, at least to a person's face. Nicknames used behind a person's back usually play up some personal idiosyncrasy, often unfavorably, and are applied primarily to males (Collier and Bricker 1970). Names used to a person's face are often kindlier and include such descriptive terms as big (*muktah*), little (bik'it), and the last baby (k'osh).

While real names may be used in school or on a job, they are not given out lightly; to know a person's real name is to have access to his soul. Indeed, newly married spouses may not tell each other, let alone their in-laws, their names for several months.

There is a conflict between the Mexican and Indian naming systems. Mexican customs and law requires the use of the father's and mother's surnames; the Indian custom requires the use of the father's Mexican and Indian surnames. These, in combination, but especially the Indian surname, carry clan connotations. Although most Indians use the Mexican naming system in school, they generally consider their real name to be the complete Indian name.

PLAY

Although play is not limited to the early childhood years, it is associated with them. Play and work are opposites. The little child, too young to understand, plays. As he grows in understanding he leaves his play behind and enters into the adult world of work.

The children's play life is active and rich. This appears to be especially true in Chamula and Zinacantan where children over the age of about six are sent off to herd the small flocks of sheep, either alone or with an older sibling. Several young shepherds often join together to form small play-groups of three or four youngsters, generally of the same sex. They are usually neighbors, often related to one another, and usually between the ages of about six and twelve. Children in the nonherding municipios also form small play-groups, usually with neighbors, and often quite close to home. Younger children spend most of their day playing within earshot of their mothers, whether near the patio or where their mother is herding the sheep.

Chamula shepherd.

Young children's play is largely exploratory, as they examine the world around them. Careful observation will stand them in good stead later, when their parents will instruct them in the minute differences among related plants and in the many other fine details of nature essential for successful farming. Observation and imitation will remain the principle learning techniques throughout life, although instructive explanations are often given. Young children manipulate many of the household objects, often using them for blocks or to roll across the uneven ground. They imitate their mothers at work, and boys also try to imitate their fathers. Parents rarely involve themselves in this play, leaving the imitation and details to the children themselves. An older child, however, who may have been assigned to watch one of the younger ones, may begin to direct the play. Parents merely lend an ear to see that children do not fight with one another and an eye to see that household property is not destroyed.

Older children's play is also highly imitative, but more likely to involve a higher degree of organization. Most of the major ceremonies are imitated; this requires the cooperative activity of several children. Family life is also imitated, and miniature houses often built. Little girls enact all the women's chores, especially food preparation and weaving. They often take a broken pot or water jug to use as a *comal* (griddle for baking tortillas), and busy themselves in making mud tortillas. Or they take some of the wisps of thread left over from their mother's weaving, construct their own looms out of sticks, and begin to make their own cloth. Boys

Household pets make good playthings, Chamula.

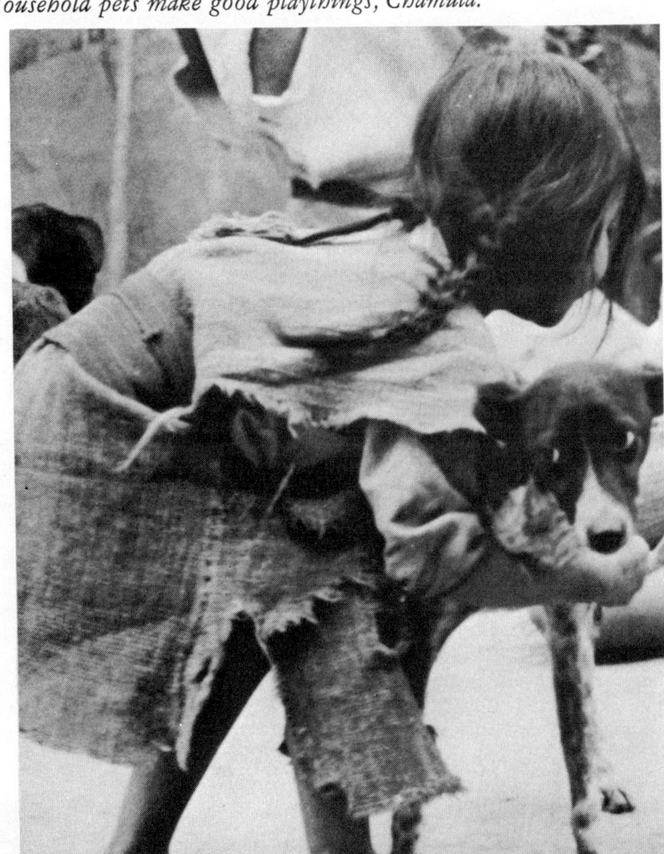

Block play with a disassembled corn grinder, Chamula.

pretend to farm. All play at going to market, becoming most involved in the etiquette of the social exchanges that take place there.

A Chamula youth recalled his play activities, which differed only slightly from those of his father:

> What I did mostly when I was a child was play. I would begin to make almost anything. Sometimes I played with mud, making little saints or houses for the saints. Sometimes several of us would get together; sometimes some were a little bigger. We'd make a house and sometimes it would fall apart; sometimes the saints wouldn't turn out right either. We'd leave them lying on the ground and when they dried we'd say they were our gods. We'd push their eyes open. When we picked them up they would fall apart. Then we'd begin to make them a house, a church. But once the house was done somebody would come along and destroy it; the next day there'd be nothing left.
>
> We really liked to make houses. They were about 3- or 4-feet high. We were all busy looking for sticks and for the potsherds which we would use for roof tiles. We'd fill in the bare places with mud; we didn't want any damn thatch for our roofs.[3] We built our houses right at the edge of the road.
>
> There was an eroded slope near the house and we dug a hole in it that remained open. It became the home of the saint's father. We dug one little cave

[3] Grass thatch was the common roofing material for all Indian homes throughout the area until the advent of truck routes in the past two decades. Now tile is considered to be both more practical and elegant, and it is used wherever people are able to truck the tiles near their homes. A few use tin, tar paper, or asbestos sheets instead, but these generally are not considered as desirable as tile.

after another, and put the saint's father there. He was a cross. We began to make little crosses. Some crosses are black near the center and white on the outside, and we had to make ours the same. We painted the center of our crosses with some shoe polish that we had hunted up. I used to make many, many things; it was because I had a restless heart.

At Easter we imitated everything we had seen the adults do; we were very happy. Our Jesus was made of mud and we tied Him onto His cross. When the mud fell apart we found sticks with which to hold Him up. There He was, propped up; we were having fun. Then we would pretend that we were speaking and praying, but we were only pretending. "Now you've died," we would say to the Christ and we would begin to weep.

Sometimes we swore at Him, imitating what should be done. We put straw on His feet and hung Him. When we took Our Lord down from the cross we threw Him on the ground and burned Him. But sometimes it went badly for us and the grass caught fire. We were frightened and tried to put out the fire. When we finished we would go home to eat.

Then we would go to look at our church again, and if it lacked walls we would put up the walls. Next we said we would build a house for the priest. Damn, did we work! We tried to build his house alongside the church, but because we tried to build it two stories high it didn't work out; we couldn't get the door right and the whole thing fell apart. "What should we do?" we asked. "Let's see, let's go to the woods. Let's find more sticks," and off we'd go. When we had gathered enough big sticks we hid them in the woods. If they had been seen they would have gone into our mothers' cooking fires. But we hid them well and had more sticks with which to build. When the new church was done some jealous child would come along and push the whole thing down.

We found a new place to build. There was a place with a few rocks and a little plain below them, and now we didn't have to plaster our walls because they were already plastered.

When we made lime we'd gather a lot of sticks and pile a lot of stones on top of them. That was my work. We'd light the fire and when we thought the stones were hot enough we'd throw water on them, and POMM! they'd split apart. But they weren't hot enough, they were only whitish inside. Sometimes we'd light the fire again, but it would go out. Sometimes we tired of that fire and began to build another somewhere else. But we never did succeed in making lime. Our intention had been to paint the walls of the church. We liked the noise of the rocks splitting, but nothing ever came of it; it was just a game.

Another time we built a fire at the edge of an open cave. We piled lots of stones up and built a huge fire, and we burnt those stones until they were very white. Then we threw water on them. We loved that sound.

Another time we began to build a very big house with three rooms. We wanted to use sand to pave it. It was going to be a king's house. We worked on it until nightfall. Our clothing was all muddied from the adobe we had been mixing. We only got the foundations done. We said it would last for a long time, but it disintegrated quickly, before our very eyes. We had used a lot of mud on the walls to make it last. It was even worse if we tried using stones. We'd use big sticks, but as soon as we stopped propping up the wall it would fall apart. No sooner had we finished one building than we would start another. That was our work every day. We played a lot.

Sometimes we would decide to make tortillas out of mud. We would put our griddle down without any fire underneath and later we would say, "Eat," but we wouldn't, of course. Then we would say, "I'm full now."

Sometimes we would decide to collect money. We would gather *chijte'* leaves. "You have to give money for the house of the Lord," we would say.

"What's it for?"

"For the priest."

One of our houses did stand for a long time, until grass began to grow at its entrance, but then it, too, fell apart. We had a dog that liked to eat the tender ears of corn. We tied him up in front of our house and said that it was his duty to see to it that nobody destroyed the House of God. And if my father scolded, well, let him scold. Sure he scolded us, and what scoldings! But the next day we did the same thing all over again.

Sometimes we would dig a little ravine across the ground and then build a bridge across it. We would look for a big bone. Nothing bothered us, we didn't even care if the bone still had some meat on it; we went ahead and used it. It was to feed the bridge, so that the black devils wouldn't come along and cut off the heads of the people who were building the bridge. We'd cover the bone with mud and put it across the ravine, with the water running below. Then we'd put boards and sticks on top, and stand on the bridge, and jump on it. PUN! PUN! That was a long time ago; I was only four or five years old then.

Then we made ourselves a truck. We had a bench in the house that was very old. We lassoed it. We loaded it with whatever had been thrown out, any old glass, or pot, or whatever, and we'd pull it around and over the bridge, making truck noises as we went. We'd boast that our car was very good and our bridge was very strong. Everything seemed good to us. We made our truck and hid it. When our father asked how our toy was doing, we weren't afraid any more; after all, we had hidden it. We were magnificent, with what we were doing! Nobody thought of bringing home any firewood. All that mattered was to play!

Sometimes my mother cooked some squash; then we would pretend to be cargo holders and make a banquet from the squash broth. We said it was honey water and invited one another to drink. We would wait until the water in the pot had cooled a bit and then we would spoon it out and drink it. Once the squash was cooked we would eat it, playing all the while.

We'd run around shouting. We found some chijte' branches, called them our truck, and mounted them, pulling them after us as we ran. What we liked was the noise they made; they sounded like a truck.

During Carnival we would play bull. One would walk like the bull and another pulled him while a third mounted him. When the bull bucked the one who was riding would fall over his horns and we would all die laughing. We would pull and pull on the animal and it would try to buck; the one who was riding would fall onto his horns.

We were all little boys. Sometimes we would make rag dolls and bury them, saying that there had been a death. There was a patch of red earth that was our graveyard. Sometimes we would find some chijte' leaves along the path and they would be our corpse. When we would revisit the grave after a few days we would find that grass had begun to sprout. Sometimes we would dig up the corpse and say that we had found the bones. The branch we had buried had already gotten bigger and had begun to put out roots, and the rags with which we had wrapped it had begun to rot. Then we would bury it again, shouting with glee. And as a part of the funeral we would drink water, pretending that it was liquor. We would get drunk. We put the water in a bottle and poured it out carefully, measuring each drink. While we drank we made faces as though the liquor was very strong.[4] Sometimes we used a dead animal for our corpse and when we dug it up there was nothing left but bones.

When we grew older we changed our games. When I was about six I looked for companions to climb with us through the forest. I looked for birds, and when I found one I felt contented. Sometimes we would find eggs. When a bigger boy

[4] Chamula children are given small amounts of liquor during ceremonial occasions even before they are weaned; these children were familiar with the taste of liquor.

Slingshot hunters, ages six and nine, Chamula.

would join us he would make a trap. He made a noose and we hid the other end of the rope where we could pull on it. We hid. When the mother bird came back to sit on her eggs we would pull on our rope and the poor bird would fall to the ground. We would play with her as we found her, still half alive. We pushed in her rib cage and liked the sound she made. She died before our eyes. Then we would throw her up in the air and she would fall back dead, and there we were, relishing the whole thing. Damn! We threw her up in the air and she died before our eyes.

Sometimes we would cut a bird open while it was still alive. We wanted to see the heart beat. We said we were doctors and wanted to see what kind of illness she had. We used a piece of broken glass for a knife; the poor bird could only open her mouth. Her heart would beat and we could see her breathe. But she was dying and hardly moving. She died before our eyes. "She can't take it any more. She died," we would say. We would bury her and then set about writing letters to her relatives to let them know that we had already buried her. Her mother would arrive with tears in her eyes. "She died," we would say, "and we have buried her."

There is another bird that makes a sound like "tic, tic." We would search for it. Sometimes we found little ones, sometimes big ones, and once we found seven baby birds. We tied their feet to make them fly like they were airplanes. Then we tied on a stick and said, "Let's see to what town they'll fly." They died and we would say that the airplane had fallen, that the gas tank had exploded.

Other times we would find a big butterfly, cut its wings, tie on a string, and let it try to fly. That's what we liked, then.

Sometimes we bought a bit of soap, mixed it with water, found a little tube, stuck it in the water, and then we began to blow until red and green bubbles came out. We would keep on blowing and they would rise to the sky. We were a little bigger then, but we didn't know how to do anything, to weed or anything; the only thing we knew was how to play.

Sometimes we made a corral for our sheep. But the sheep were nothing more than a pile of droppings we had gathered. We shaped them and said that we had a lot of sheep. Sometimes we would pretend to be the sheep. We would lie on the ground and begin to eat the grass. We were all eating away at the grass, and you can imagine how we all looked; it was funny!

If we began to feel hungry we would take out the tortillas we carried and eat them while we played. We would all agree to put our tortillas together and then break them into smaller pieces. Everyone carried a tortilla hidden in his clothing. Then we would pretend that we were eating chicken..

Sometimes we'd pretend that a baby was going to be born. We would find a little worm or an insect. "The baby has been born," we'd say and put the animals up to boil. "It's for the baby that's going to be born." We had a little saint, and we delighted in saying, "For the baby that was just born." Then we would eat the meat and some tortillas. We would take a pot out of the house and sometimes some hot coals, too, and cook on the porch. While we were waiting for the food to cook we would say, "It will be good when our meal

Anatomy of a bird, Chamula.

is cooked." We divided up the food and filled some bottles with water; that was our liquor. Then we would begin to drum, but our drums were the bottles that we banged on the ground. PUM! PUM! PUM! on the ground.

Sometimes we played at being horses. We would mount each other and ride around; sometimes the horse was weak and fell down. We would use some old drinking glasses for horseshoes and make the prints show on the ground. We would race our horses. Sometimes a horse was very angry and threw the rider over his head and the rider cried with pain. So many things occurred to us.

Sometimes we would try standing on our heads and then we would turn over. Sometimes we would whirl around, pretending that we were drunk, and we would begin to sing. We would get dizzy from so much turning and begin to vomit.

Sometimes we pretended to be important men, saying, "I'm *Regidor*," "I'm *Alcade*," "I'm *Alferez*." Sometimes we would begin to divide up the work, preparing to pass a cargo on to someone just as we saw the adults do. We would go to the door of the house shouting, "Bread, bread!" We would carry a paper for the owner of the house, appointing him to the cargo. We were all shouting, imitating the noise of cannons. We looked for some cornstalks to serve as the office holders' staffs. We also imitated how we kneel in my town [during a swearing-in ceremony]. We would cut the cornstalks, kneel, and shout our oaths of fidelity.

"O.K., go on," the new office holder would say; then we would move on. When we arrived at the appropriate spot one of us would have the staff of office ready. We would also look for some sticks that were a little bent; we would string some wire on them and pretend they were musical instruments. Sometimes we would look for an old guitar. When our instruments were ready we would begin to play. The music sounded out and the new office holder danced for us. Damn! We were so little! We would eat and drink and set off firecrackers; sometimes we got a stomachache.

Then we would pretend that there had been a fight and we went to seek justice from the President. I pretended to be the President and everyone came to me, telling what had happened. "It is good that you have come to tell me." I would jail the culprit in our steambath, and the one who had been wronged was happy again. The ones who had begun the suit said, "We buried a corpse and asked him [the culprit] to help with some money, but he didn't want to give any, and that's why we began to fight." I responded that it was a grave matter and that I would jail him. The complainants insisted that he be jailed for several hours. When the hours had passed I let him out, saying that he should never do it again. I would say, "You have to pay a fine. You have to pay 1000 pesos." Then he would begin to gather chijte' leaves until he had a lot of money.

Sometimes we would sell refreshments. We would fill bottles with water and file down some sticks for candles. The one who bought the candles would begin to pray inside his house. I sold the candles.

Sometimes when we pretended to pray, someone would hide in a chijte' tree and begin to complain that his prayers weren't being answered at all, or perhaps just a little. Then the patient would thank the one who was doing the praying and give him some money, asking if that was all he was going to do. The curer would respond that something was still lacking for him to be completely cured. Then he would begin to prepare his candles, deciding what kind of candles should be used. He would say that we had to use 5-cent candles. The patient would buy his candles from me; I sold and sold my candles.

Sometimes someone would decide that it was a serious case of envy and that it could spread to others. We would begin to return the envy. We would blow on the patient and then begin to say that now our prayers were being heard. The patient thanked him and the curer left the house; the patient continued lying there on the ground covered with a little tunic. Another would ask what time we were going to bathe him and the curer would say, "Right now." So we would begin to give him his steambath while others prepared the clothing in which he would dress afterward. But we only said we would bathe him. We looked for soap, and with a palm leaf we would begin to warm him. Then we would pretend that night was coming, and he would lay down to sleep. "Tonight my wife will sleep alone," he said. He would fall asleep and we would pretend that the devil had come, and we would make a lot of noise. "Eeeeee," we cried, and everybody hid inside their tunics to scare him away.

Sometimes we pretended that it was fiesta time and we would make atole, but we really just mixed mud. We built a fire and put the atole into a little jug to cook. Pretty soon it would boil. We would add water and sugar, but the sugar was just dried earth. Sometimes we made coffee. There was some very black earth that we used and our coffee turned out very black. Then we would look for some bread; our bread was chijte' leaves or sometimes little loaves of mud.

During the time of All Saints we would await our dead. We cut lots of marigolds. We made a table with a board and four sticks; we made a banquet of chijte' leaves and meat. We would use worms or something for the meat, but whatever it was, it was our meat, and we hunted for it enthusiastically. Then we would begin to weep, calling to our dead ones, "Come to eat, come to eat." We would go to the graveyard, carrying our mud atole, and we would pour it over the grave and leave it there so that the dead could eat. Then we would go to buy oranges. We found some juicy leaves and said they were sugarcane; we also used the long fruit of a plant that grows here. For oranges we used *k'at'ix* fruits. We would leave all of those things on the grave. We were very smart! And we would kneel and pretend to weep.

That was our work when we were growing up.

When I got a little older, I stopped playing quite so much. Sometimes we found some tall trees and climbed them without thinking that we might fall. My companions climbed up and so did I. We didn't care whether we fell or not; we weren't afraid of anything. And we'd swing from the branches. We'd chase after one another in the branches. We thought we were squirrels. If someone didn't dare climb up we would tease him, saying he was a coward, a woman. And if he still wouldn't climb we would say that they didn't put his navel cord in a tree when he was born, that maybe they had buried it somewhere or that a dog had eaten it.

Sometimes we thought we were rabbits and began to jump like rabbits. Some of the children would come to hunt the rabbits while we hid in the tall grass. When they found us we began to shout. The grass hurt our faces as we crawled through it. Once something bit me on the feet and I thought, "What snake has bitten me?" I began to burn some moss; I cooked it in a pot and cured the snake-bite. When my foot got better I went out to play again.

We jumped across the ravines. We liked to leap across because our hearts felt that they were flying. We were very happy.

Sometimes we would roll down a hillside. Or we would mash up some little red fruits and take them for refreshments. We would sell the drinks. Then we would drink, even though it wrenched our mouths.

Sometimes we would race one another. Some could run very far, but others would lag behind or throw themselves down at the side of the path. Sometimes we would jump on the back of a bigger boy (the jumping boy makes a tumpline of his hands), and he would begin to spin around and around; when he fell, we did too, and our noses began to bleed. "Don't cry, or your mother will scold," we would say. Even though I got hurt, I didn't care. I would start playing right away.

There is a ravine where we played. I would walk along the edge and then jump to the bottom. Sometimes we would take a board and slide down, or we would use a smooth stick. Two or three of us would sit on the same board or pole. Sometimes we looked for straw, saying that it was our truck. When we tired we would sit and think of what else we could do, and if some wanted to go home we would tell them to stay so that we could all go on playing together.

It was hard for us to stop playing; we always found something to do. If we found a big hole in the ground we would find a forked stick and while one jumped over the hole, using the stick to help him, others would try to turn it. Or one would jump on the stick while another pulled him along, leaving furrows in the ground. We said they were tire marks. Sometimes the stick gave out and the one who was riding it fell; we would shout with laughter. But it really hurt our hands because we were still little.

Sometimes we would mount the sheep; they were our horses. Sometimes I couldn't get on. The boy who was mounted would spur the horse on and it would race away.

Sometimes we hid among the pots in the house, and we would frighten the one who came to find us. We thought we were devils. If we found a rolled up petate we would hide in it, or sometimes we hid under the bed. When someone was caught he would help the devil find another boy. When everybody was found we would hide all over again.

If it started to rain we didn't pay any attention; we would run around in the water. If there was a big puddle nearby we would go to play there. We would take off our clothing and wade in. We bathed ourselves and wet our clothing. We shouted with glee. My father would get angry. "Why did you let yourselves get wet?" he would say, but we didn't pay any attention, and soon we would be outside again. We liked it when the wind blew hard. We held out our arms and said to the wind, "Come, wind!"

There was a little tree growing nearby and we liked to climb it and swing in the branches; we didn't think that we might fall. Now the tree has dried up.

Sometimes we would make a flag and fly it. We tied a cloth to the top of a long stick and ran with it. Sometimes we would strip a chijte' branch of all its leaves except for a few at the top and use it for our flag.

Sometimes we dressed in clothing that was used in ancient times; we would dress in monkey (max) clothes.[5] We would get dressed and shriek like the monkey. Everyone would look at us running about in our monkey clothing with our flag.

We made a guitar out of a board; we would put some wire on it and begin to play. There was also an ancient harp of my grandfather's. We played and played on it until our hands hurt from so much strumming. We played all day, and at night we would sleep soundly. We were all boys playing together, but sometimes we were joined by my little sisters [cousins]. There was a girl who lived nearby, but since we didn't play with her she was left all alone. We would see her wandering around the edge of her house, singing and playing alone.

I liked to play with squash flowers. They were my radio; I made sounds with them. Or I would tie a bee or some other flying thing inside the flower and it would buzz; it was my music. I did that when I was a child, but when I was bigger I didn't have many opportunities to play; my companions were all gone. So I began to work, too, and play was almost forgotten.

[5] The max (monkey) costume is worn on certain ceremonial occasions. Although it contains many Spanish elements, an essential item is a peaked cap made of the fur of the howler monkey, which lives in the jungle. In pre-Columbian times the max was a god of entertainment (Blom 1956).

In the nonherding tribes boys seem to be about as free in their play. A middle-aged man from Chenalho remembered:

When I was little we used to play around my house, my cousins and I. We were about the same age. We'd go into the woods, we'd race, we'd look for fruits to eat, we'd wander through the cornfields. On some occasions someone would be a deer and the others would hunt him. We'd use cornstalks or sticks for rifles; they broke easily. With those same rifles we'd hunt mosquitoes and other insects. We'd also make cane arrows with which to hunt butterflies. We were always looking for some animal to kill. We spent our days in the milpas or we'd wander through the forest with our little machetes, looking for something to play with.

We pretended to ride horses. We'd find a good-sized stick, tie a rope to one end, and begin to ride it around the outside of the house [in imitation of ceremonial races]. When any little girls played with us they would wait at the finish lines. We would drink, as is done in the fiestas. Our liquor was water. We would find some old glasses and measure out the liquor. We would make two teams, just as is done in the fiestas. But we didn't count the number of turns we took; we just kept on until we got tired. I was perhaps six or seven.

Sometimes we would swing ourselves from the rafters. We might hang from ropes or leather thongs, whatever was at hand. We never fell down, but if we did we just laughed. My little boys do the same now.

We built play houses with roofs of corn leaves. We made them big enough so that two or three could crouch inside. If the houses stood for two days that was a long time. We would build a fire in the hearth. Sometimes it was a good-sized fire; sometimes it burnt the house. And we would drink; we would fill a bottle with water.

When the girls played with us they would make tortillas or use corn leaves for tortillas. That's when we went out to hunt. But our deer were only lumps of earth which we cooked up in clay pots. We went off, but never very far from home, while the women waited for us, entertaining themselves. We would bring them firewood, but our wood was only twigs mixed with earth. After finishing our meal we pretended to go out to work. We planted the little lumps of earth. We took our little play hoes and went to the milpa just like my little boys do now. They work, too, but it's just for moments and then it's nothing but a game. If we were just boys playing together without any girls we would make our meal anyhow, and any one of us would serve it. There were plenty of us, sometimes seven or eight.

Sometimes we were bulls; we used vines for ropes. We would use the vines to tie our feet together and then try to jump; we would fall to the ground. Or we would race one another to see who could run fastest. We were covered with dirt from all our playing.

We also played hide-and-seek in the cornfields. We took turns at hiding and searching. When the seeker found someone he would try to pull him out and we would laugh.

We also played with the dogs. We would tie them up and pretend that we were going to slaughter them. Or we would load them up with cargo as though they were horses. We used rags for saddle blankets.

Sometimes we looked for flowers for the Day of the Dead. We made our little clay saints and decorated them with flowers. We knelt in prayer and drank liquor, sometimes two or three bottles. And we wept. We did that on any day of the year, but on the real Day of the Dead we didn't play because we had to respect the souls of the dead. When we played we made our banquet of earth. We used whatever we found for pots: avocado skins, potsherds. We cooked squash and atole; we imitated whatever we saw. And we prayed. First the dead ate, then we ate.

Girls tell much the same tales about their play as do boys, whether they herd sheep or not. A young Chamula woman remembered:

Sometimes we would make toys out of clay, jugs, or cooking pots. Then we would make a fire and try to heat them, but they always fell apart. Or we would make little horses [ceremonial objects]. Sometimes we made dolls out of old rags and maybe sticks that we found lying around. At harvest time I would use the cornsilk for hair; if it was a girl, I would braid her hair. Sometimes I made dolls that were ready to give birth. I stuffed them with rags. When the baby was ready to be born I would untie the doll's belt so that she could give birth. Once the baby was born I made the doll carry it.

Since we saw how adults prayed at the well, we would dig a little well, tie two sticks into a cross, and pretend to pray with our play candles. But one time a little friend had just kneeled down to pray when she fell in and got all wet. That ended that game!

Once in a while we would pretend to be curers. We would take the patient's pulse and then diagnose a serious illness. "Well, it seems the patient was bitten by a lizard!" We were really very funny. We would begin to drink, but it was just water. We would portion it out and oblige everyone to have some. Then we would pass out some more. Pretty soon we were all pretending to be drunk.

Sometimes we pretended that our child had died, and we buried it. We had a special graveyard. We pretended to be grieving deeply. We invited the curer to save the child, but she said that he was too sick. Then he died, right there in front of the curer. We used the tortillas we had brought along to eat. We put up crosses and threw water over the grave. Who knows what the water was for, but we imitated what we had seen the adults do.

Sometimes we would make houses, but only when we played with the boys. To perform the housewarming ceremony we needed a guitar; one of the boys once sneaked one out of his house. He began to play the guitar inside the play-house. Then it began to pour and the guitar became unglued.

While the boys looked for birds we girls would build a fire and prepare the meal. We would then serve it, some of us contributing more tortillas than others. After all, we were celebrating our housewarming. By the next day the house would be in ruins. If one of the children had a milpa nearby we would tell him to bring us some fresh corn. Once, when one of the boys had gotten us a lot of corn, and big ears, too, his mother came along. Imagine how he felt! He had simply done what we had told him to do; he had pulled up the corn, stalks and all.

When his mother came over to us we told her what he had done. We had already planned that we would chase after him and pretend that we couldn't catch him. That's what we did, and he fled, shrieking, into the forest; he dropped all his corn. We gathered it and showed it to his mother; she said he would get a good beating when he got home. After that he said he would never do it again.

But that didn't stop us. We just looked for another corn field and pulled up the stalks to get at the corn ears. We made various things from that fresh corn, such as tortillas and tamales. When we had finished cooking we invited our girlfriends to have one or two. One of the girls was especially clever, and she got us everything we needed to cook on. But when we got caught we got scolded.

Or we took boards and slid down the hill with them. Sometimes we hurt our hands that way. It seems nothing was good for play.

We also liked to climb trees and pick the fruit. I always went with the same girl. We'd decide to climb and go up to the top. Then she would say that we should climb down. She was bigger and got right down, but I couldn't. When she got to the ground she would break off some of the branches so that it was even harder for me to get down. I cried and cried until my brother's wife came to get me. Sometimes my own friends annoyed me.

Another time when we quarreled was when we spotted a nest. She said to take it, but I wanted to leave the birds alone. She grabbed it and we quarreled. Sometimes we didn't speak to each other for two or three days, but then the anger would pass and we would play together. But we would do other things; for instance, we would make slingshots, but since we really didn't know how to make them, they would break. She finally made one that worked, but I never did.

When there were other children we would help one another finish the spinning we had been given, and then we would start to play. Sometimes we played at being cows or sheep and butted one another. Or we would jump across small ravines or spray one another with water. We pretended that we were asleep, and the others would spray us; we especially liked that when the sun was very hot.[6] We learned our games from one another.

Sometimes we played hide-and-seek. Those who wanted to hide did, while the others looked for them. The one who searches is the devil. When we were found we would run away and see if the devil could find us. Sometimes she would grab us, carry us over to some bushes and dump us there. Sometimes I would be the devil but I was never any good at it.

Sometimes we would just race after one another to see who could run the fastest. The bigger girls always won; then they would laugh at us. When we caught up they would throw us to the ground.

A middle-aged woman from Chenalho recalled:

I remember that when I was little I played a lot. We made dolls for ourselves and gathered flowers. We made the dolls into saints and made little altars for ourselves. We constructed little houses and set up the altars. Sometimes we made our saints of sticks, sometimes of corn cobs. We dressed them in rags. We fashioned belts for them and wrapped their heads. We formed beautiful little heads for them. Sometimes we made crosses, but we were scolded when we did that. We were told that if we made a cross Mama would die; it was all right if we just made little saints and adorned them. We didn't kneel either; we just pretended that we were kneeling in prayer. By then I was big enough to carry my baby brother.

Sometimes we dressed our dolls and looked for parents for them; we made them carry their babies. Then we picked some flowers so that our little dolls could have their playthings. We would find some reddish leaves for their faces. "Look how beautiful our little girl is," we would say.

Sometimes we were just two or three, but sometimes we played with my cousins, the children of an aunt who lived nearby, and then there were many of us. They taught us many things. We would pretend to be other people. "Older brother, brother-in-law," we would greet one another. "Come sister-in-law, come Madame," we would answer.

Sometimes we found berries to eat. Sometimes we pretended to be grown women. We would boil the berries, or at least their juice, in a little clay pot. We made tortillas, sometimes out of mud, sometimes out of leaves. "The tortillas are ready," we would say, laying them out to bake.

If we found very thick mud we would make some pots for ourselves. "Look, I'm making a pot in which to cook my corn," I would say. When the mud had

---

[6] When this woman was a child both boys and girls wore heavy woolen clothing. Now many girls wear cotton blouses with their woolen skirts.

dried we would bake the pots, but they always fell apart in the heat. That was our work then.

Sometimes we sneaked a pot out of the house, but when Mama found her pot all stained red from the berry juice she would ask, "Have you no shame? Look how you've used my pot for a toy!" After that scolding we would look for a pot that was already cracked and hide it away for our own use.

"Now we're eating *mole* [meat in a heavy spicy sauce]," we would say, and pretend to eat, but it was just the berries and our make-believe tortillas. We pretended to put the food into our mouths, but we really threw it to the ground. We used green berries for the meat and the juice of the red berries for the sauce. Of course, we never played that way inside the house, just nearby. We couldn't go far from home because we were girls; Mama never wanted us to play with boys.

Sometimes my little sister and I fought. We scolded and hit one another. If my sister liked one of my toys, if a doll looked pretty to her, she would take it away from me. If I liked one of her's I would take it. One would hit and the other would cry and then hit back.

Sometimes Mama would spoil some thread or some would be left over from a piece she had woven. I would gather it and spin it again, imitating her. Then I would try to weave, but my cloth came out all wrong. I didn't have a real loom, just a bit of this and that. "My weaving won't come out, it's no good," I said.

Sometimes we raced and tagged one another. Sometimes we hid. That was our work, to play. Sometimes we all piled up on top of one another. Sometimes we hid in a great big urn that stood inside the house, or underneath a bed. But we never climbed up to the rafters like the boys did. Sometimes we found one another, but sometimes, if we weren't found, we would try to scare the searcher. "HAU!" we would shout. We thought that was very funny.

Sometimes we played hide-and-seek in the woods. Sometimes we found one another, sometimes not. If we weren't found we would try to scare one another. We would first play inside the house, but when we had used up all the hiding places we would go to the woods. When we couldn't think of any more places to hide the game would be over. One child would do the seeking until she got tired.

"Now it's your turn to look." "You hide now," we would say, and another child would start looking. But we always wanted the best searcher to do the seeking.

"Let's hide! Who's going to hide?"

"I'll hide."

"No, I'll hide."

"No, you hide, hurry up and hide," we said.

"Then you'll have to look for me."

"Yes." And we would hide. "Well, go away. You're not going to see where we hide," we would say.

"Go far away."

"We're watching to make sure you don't peek."

But sometimes we were naughty and peeked from between our hands. Then we could be very clever and find the children quickly. Sometimes the children hid far away and it was hard to find them. When we got tired of playing one thing we would start playing something else.

Once we began learning to work we stopped playing.

When the children play hide-and-seek, the purpose is to hide well and then to scare the one who comes searching. The first or the last to be caught may sometimes be "it" during the next round, but often it is the child who volunteers for this role and who may take it over and over again. There are other feats of strength and daring, as the children compete to see such things as who can run fastest, carry another child on a tumpline made of his clasped hands, jump over a small ravine, climb a small cliff, or otherwise manage a particularly dangerous trail. Games of marbles and tops are also played, primarily by the boys and especially around the schoolhouse. Home-made tops and small fruits may sometimes be substituted for the store-bought items. In Oxchuc there is also a game for pitching small stones in which either a straight line or a more intricate figure is drawn on the ground. In the former case, the one to throw his stone closest to the line wins; in the latter, the aim is to get the stone into one of the circles. Small coins may be used, in which case the winner takes all.

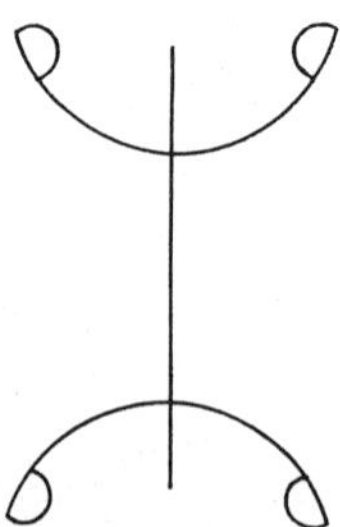

Pervading all talk of play, however, is the firm belief that play and work are opposites and that all of one's time should be spent gainfully. All informants expressed regret at having "wasted" their time in play once they had begun to do chores, and only one, the youngest and still an adolescent, expressed any regret at having had to curtail his play activities.

3 / Middle and later childhood

Whatever small amount of age-grading occurs among the Indians depends primarily upon a child's ability to work. Children who are beginning to do chores at about the age of five or six are still called kerem (boy), achix (girl, Tzeltal), or tseb (girl, Tzotzil). After about the age of ten or eleven, when children can carry out their chores competently and assume considerable responsibility for their work, they are called *mukul kerem* or *mukul achix* in Tzeltal (*mukul* meaning big); *muk'tah kerem* or *muk'tah tseb* in Tzotzil (*muk'tah* meaning big). Males are generally considered *winik* (man) after about the age of twenty when they can work with all the strength and competence of men, whether or not they marry. But it is only with the birth of her first child that a girl is called *antz* (woman); women who do not have children continue to be called mukul achix (Tzeltal) or muk'tah tseb (Tzotzil) for life. Variants of these terms include the practice in parts of Chamula of calling women muk'tah tseb until they have had several children and long after they have left their in-laws to form homes of their own; the practice of calling older, unmarried women *yijil tseb* (old maid) in Chenalho; and the concept of three rather than two childhood stages in Zinacantan, where the terms bik'it kerem or bik'it tseb are extended until about the age of ten. The terms muk'tah kerem or muk'tah tseb are used to cover the period when the child gains competency, and the term *sva'lej* used for the teen years (Vogt 1969:182).

LEARNING TO BE AN ADULT

The ideal child is hardworking, obedient, and responsible; he does not waste his time in play. Parents begin to teach their children to work nearly from infancy in much of Chamula and Zinacantan, and by the age of six elsewhere. A toddler may be given a fistful of corn to throw to the chickens when his mother goes to feed them, or he may be given a soft, leafy branch with which to shoo them away. Little is expected of him, but he is encouraged to imitate his mother. As soon as a little girl begins to imitate her mother's motions in making tortillas she is given her own stool, a piece of plastic, and a miniature wad of dough; any tortillas she actually forms are placed on the griddle along with her mother's, to be fed to the dogs if they are not good enough for people. By the age of four or five a little girl should be making tortillas to be eaten by the rest of the family, although she is not yet expected to reach over the fire to handle them on the griddle.

As soon as children show that they can follow simple instructions, perhaps at about three, they are given errands to perform, such as to bring a stick of wood to the hearth. Parents state that they expect their two-year-olds to obey, but if a very young child does not obey or leave his play it is assumed that he is too young to understand. A parent may request something several times, only to be ignored; he then concludes that the child is too immature to understand him, at least at that moment. Nor is he likely to help the child perform the chore unless asked for help; the parent's first response is likely to be to offer verbal encouragement and perhaps some instructions, but not to go to the child's aid until he becomes particularly distressed. Parents relish their children's precocity, but they expect relatively little of them during this early (ch'in or bik'it) stage. Girls are expected to begin to carry a small gourd or miniature jug and to accompany their mothers to get water at about the age of four, and all children are expected to fetch and carry small objects near at hand, to shell a bit of corn, and to feed the chickens. But parents

First lesson in felting.

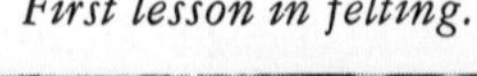

Ready to go for water, Chamula.

rarely scold if children's attention is drawn away from their work, feeling that they are too young to know any better. It is only after the age of six or seven that they are likely to scold when children show themselves to be more involved with their play than with the work at hand.

A four-year-old Oxchuquero, the oldest child in his household, was sliding down a pile of burlap sacks with three other children ranging in age from two to five. They giggled lustily as they played. The boy's mother placed his thirteen-month-old sister in a hammock about ten yards away and called for him to swing it. He made no response, as though he had not heard. She called to him several more times, each time more insistently until, after the fifth call, he left the group to swing the hammock. After just two pulls on the rope he was distracted by his noisy playmates and ran to join them. The infant began crying and the mother went to swing the hammock.

Disobedience is never consciously tolerated, although the definition of disobedience becomes stricter as the child grows older. Young children are expected to lack understanding, and allowance is made for this. However, it is stated that children may never strike their parents.

One mother insisted that her three-year-old daughter never hit her, even as the child was striking her gently with a closed fist to protest some eyedrops she was administering. This same mother had shortly before disowned a fully grown son for striking her when he was drunk and, therefore, not expected to be aware of his behavior.

The younger a child and the more dependent, the more he appears to be enjoyed by his parents. Infants are cuddled, carressed, and kissed; nothing is expected in return. As children become more independent and more capable of caring for themselves, parents raise their expectations and become more impatient with noncompliance or inadequate performance. Little children may not "understand" and be forgiven for any inattention or breach in behavior, but after about the age of six or seven, when a child has shown himself capable of helping at least a little, expectations soar and tempers grow short. Once a child has shown himself able to "understand" he is considered at fault when he does not.

Helping Mama carry firewood, Oxchuc.

Boys are sent to work alongside their fathers, although little is expected of them at first in strength or attention span. It is customary for a man to teach his son the names of all the plants and their uses and to show his boy all the techniques of farming. The son must listen attentively and imitate as best he can, working opposite his father on the same row, although many times during the day he may forget and begin to play or daydream. When this happens his father should gently redirect his attention to the work, although many men resort to scolding, even striking, their sons. When several children accompany their father to the fields the temptation to play may become irresistible. Yet parents take their children to the fields not only to teach them, but also for the labor they contribute.

When a boy shows himself able to farm he should be given a small plot of land for his own where land is plentiful, as in Chenalho; his earnings are his own, to be used to buy clothing and school supplies and to contribute to the family. Where land is not easily available boys begin to accompany their fathers or older brothers, and later to go alone, to work as day laborers in the lowland cornfields or coffee plantations. They are allowed to keep at least part of their earnings to meet some of their personal expenses and to save toward their marriages.[1] In Amatenango, however, it is neither expected that boys farm on their own nor gain any economic independence until well after marriage; in turn, their parents are expected to meet all their needs and to pay for their particularly expensive weddings.

While children are proud of their growing skills, they find that learning to work is not easy and most have ambivalent feelings. Not only do children have to give up much of their active play, but many of the tasks are painful or very tiring, if not actually frightening at first. Children may begin to carry with a tumpline in play, but within a few years, often at about the age of six or so, they are given bundles to carry which they find quite heavy and unmanageable; they may be expected to carry them for considerable distances. The child first undertaking such an endeavor may be encouraged by his parents and soothed verbally, "Come along, don't cry, we'll be home soon, I'll give you an orange (or some other reward, usually food) when we get there. See how big my little one is, he's carrying like a big person." But rarely will the parent, himself far more burdened than the child, help him with the load. Older siblings are far less patient. A Chamula youth remembered:

> When I went for firewood with my mother, I would bring back my own little bundle. When I went alone I was afraid: I never knew when the bundle was arranged well or when it would fall apart. If my older brothers told me it was good I said it was good; if they said it was bad I repeated that it was bad, but I really didn't know anything. If my bundle was heavy I would trail behind crying. I was also pretty small when I began going for water. I remember that I cried a lot and broke the little jugs I carried. I never went alone; I was afraid of the horses that pastured nearby.

An old man of the same tribe, remembering how he learned to work, recalled:

> When I was little all I knew how to do was to shell a bit of corn and feed the chickens. But I was afraid: The chickens would jump at me and I'd cry.

---

[1] Present costs of an Indian marriage range between 300 and 10,000 pesos, depending upon the tribe and the reputation of the girl and her family.

The turkeys were worse, especially the toms. I remember that my big sister had a turkey then. I was so frightened. When I went to the yard to relieve myself, dammit, that animal didn't let me finish. I complained to my mother that I didn't even know what animal it was that was giving me such a hard time; she told me it was a turkey. I was very little then to be frightened of a turkey. It was hard to shell the corn, but my mother didn't insist too much when she saw I couldn't do it. When we are little we never take life seriously. As long as our belly is full, nothing else matters.

When I was very tiny my mother would sometimes ask me to bring her a stick of wood for the fire but I wasn't even able to carry it; I would drag it in after me. Then, when I was bigger, I began to help her carry wood to market. I walked like a drunkard, crying from the exertion and from the pain of going barefoot on the stony trails. She would laugh at me when I fell, and then take the little bundle of sticks and carry them herself, saying I was too little to do anything yet. It was a joke to her. And all I wanted to do was play!

Once my father found work mixing mud [clay] at a brickworks where the INI stands now; it was a large pasture then. He took me along to gather horse droppings to mix in with the mud. But I was frightened of all the big animals and cried a lot. Most of the time I didn't do anything; I just waited until he was near. He would get angry because he paid 25 cents a day for the use of that field and at most I'd fill up only two or three baskets.

Later he sent me alone to San Cristobal to look for work, but since I didn't speak any Spanish it was very hard. Sometimes I would just stand in a doorway to see if anybody would take pity on me and ask what I wanted. When I did find work, I'd get 10 or 20 *centavos*, maybe 25. They didn't pay much in those days; they didn't pay enough. In the fincas, then, you could earn 60 centavos a day, and that was pretty good. In my father's time 3 pesos a week was good pay. When I sold wood with my mother, between us we'd earn perhaps 20 centavos.

Sometimes someone would have me weed his cornfield. I might even get three *reales* {37½ centavos} for that, and I was happy because that meant several days' work. Sometimes I would find work hauling stones or cleaning the streets, or I might be sent from house to house gathering ashes (used for dying the cloth of women's skirts). I learned a lot, going from house to house, and little by little I lost my fear; it became easier for me to find work. But it was never as easy then as it is now.

My father showed me how to work in the milpa. He told me what to do and how to measure. He always explained things to us, saying when the space between the cornstalks was too big or too small, and that if we weeded too deeply we would leech the topsoil.

When I was bigger I decided to go to the finca. I was only about fifteen then, but they gave me a man's work; I became a man at the finca.

His sons described much the same history in learning to work.

A man from Chenalho remembered:

When I was about eight I began to farm. I remember that it was hard. I didn't want to work; I wanted to keep on playing. Sometimes I would weed half a row, sometimes a whole row, but it was hard to finish. I got scolded every once in a while.

My father showed me how to farm. He told me what to do and how to do it, to do it the way he did. It was hard. In those days the hoes were made by blacksmiths, and the edges gave out very quickly. We didn't have metal files either, and we had to sharpen them with stones. It was very tiring. Sometimes my father told us why we should do something a certain way. If we said we couldn't do it well he told us to do it well anyhow. But if we didn't pay attention he would get angry and hit us. He hit us with the hoe and made us cry; he had to draw our attention back to our work pretty often.

My father would do four or five rows, for he worked quickly, but my brother and I would barely finish one. Then he would come to help us finish. When we cut down the overgrowth {preparing a new field}, we used a scythe. We each had a little one, and little by little we learned to mow. Before then we used our little machetes and did whatever we could to help my father. But we got bored easily and began playing.

When I was about ten years old my father gave me my own little milpa. It was only 3 or 4 armlengths in each direction and I only worked on it for short spells in the morning or afternoon because I had to go to school. But little by little I made it bigger. I used what I earned to buy my hat and a few other things. Then I began trading a bit. We'd go along the main trails to buy bananas. Sometimes I carried sixty, seventy even one hundred bananas. When I was a little stronger I could carry more, and with my earnings I bought my clothing and my blanket. Sometimes I went alone, sometimes with a friend. We would go to Chalchihuitan. We left early, slept there, and returned the next day. My companions were big, but I tagged along with them; I was perhaps eleven. My father let me go and I liked it; at the least I could eat bananas. With the money I earned I bought my clothing and was able to save a few cents. By the time I got married I had a little money put away.

Little by little I learned to make *chicha* [fermented sugar-water]; that helped my business. Sometimes I would carry two or three *zontles* [loads of four hundred] of bananas every week [on pack animals]. Once I began making chicha I was able to sell near home. I made good chicha, which is why it sold so easily; it wasn't necessary to drink much in order to get drunk. Sometimes I would sell three or four large jugs in just two or three hours. Then we had money to spend, but we still suffered. I could keep all the money I made for myself; I didn't have to give any of it to my parents. And, of course, I kept working my little cornfield.

Girls begin to work with their mothers at about the age of six, although they, too, are not expected to perform in a truly adult way. At first they are given a series of short tasks, and their mothers are willing to redo what they have done too ineptly. Thus a girl may be given a piece of clothing to wash and after she has tired of scrubbing it her mother may take over. But the willingness to redo soon wanes, and the girl may be scolded and prodded to keep scrubbing every time she complains. She is more likely to be given a baby's soiled shirts or some work clothes to wash, not her father's fiesta clothing, so that inept performance is of little importance. In a similar fashion girls begin to take on all the housekeeping and child-caring tasks of their mothers.

In much of Chamula and Zinacantan they begin very young and learn largely through imitation, with scoldings reserved for obvious inadequacies or laziness. In the other areas, where little is expected until about the age of six, the training appears to be harsher. Mothers are more likely to use corporal methods of instruction and punishment. A girl of about eight who is having trouble forming tortillas is likely to have her mother grab a semibaked tortilla from the hot comal and rub it into her hands until she cries from pain, as her mother says, "Your hand has been very lazy [naughty]; it doesn't want to work." In this way the girl is expected to learn to form her tortillas well and to overcome her fear of the hot comal. In the same way her mother is likely to later hit her hands with the wooden crossbars

Six-year-old girl caring for baby brother, Oxchuc.

of the loom to insure that she learns to weave well, or to prick her fingers with a needle to insure her success at embroidery. When a girl has particular trouble in learning to weave, prayers may be intoned to the female saints. In Chenalho, the Virgin of the Rosary is appealed to in particular; the mother may pass the girl's hands along the saint's brocaded clothing and across her eyes.

Although corporal teaching methods are common in many of the municipios, not all women follow them; some dislike inflicting pain on children, feel it accomplishes nothing, and prefer patient explanation and kindliness as means of instruction. Like fathers with their sons, women seldom praise their daughters for working well, since good work is expected, but are likely to point out shortcomings or to scold.

When a woman leaves the house to work alongside her husband in the fields, the girl may either accompany her, thus learning some of the elements of farming herself, or she may be left at home, fully in charge of the hearth and the younger children. Although she is expected to do all the housework when left alone (at least from about the age of eight), she often has some time for play. It is considered cruel to leave a young child (under the age of about six) at home alone.

One Chamula mother resolved the problem of caring for her two-and-a-half-year-old daughter when she went on hour-long trips for water by tying the family dog near the house to provide companionship for the girl. A year later she left the little girl alone with the dog for several hours at a time when she went to San Cristobal. Her neighbors considered this perfectly adequate care for the child. Children of two and four may be left alone in each other's company for much of the day; of course, no work is expected from such young children, and some food is set out for them if no more responsible person is expected to return home for several hours. But young children are never left by themselves after dark, which is a frightening time for many.

A woman from Chenalho, the oldest in her family, remembered how she learned to work:

I was about four years old and I remember when we were working at a finca. Papa would say to me, "You cut some coffee, too," and I would help him gather the berries. Even the little I could gather was a great help. Mama was more agile and didn't need any help.

"Work hard, work hard," Papa said to me. "My little daughter is very helpful." Of course, I didn't work all day, just for short spells, just when my heart told me to help. The rest of the time I played with my baby sister under the coffee bushes. "Come here," my father would call to me, "Here are some low branches, come help gather the berries."

I remember that when I was a little bigger and we were back home again, my mother would scold me when I didn't do things well. She spanked me once for spilling some water and Papa said, "Well, your mother mistreats you a lot. I think I'll send you off to be a servant." My grandmother said, "She mistreats you a lot. How can you do things well yet, you're so little?" I remember, like a dream, that my grandmother took me and was going to leave me at a ladino's house. I didn't want to go. It all happened because Mama beat me. I had spilled some water and she wanted to use me like a mop, to clean up all the mud. She treated us all like that.

Papa also scolded my sister and me because we were women and would go off with our husbands when we were grown. But he never scolded to make me work harder.

When I was a little bigger I was put in charge of the house. "Put up the beans to cook," Mama would say. "Warm a jug of water. Wash the corn well." I did all of that; it was my work. But still I played; I was really quite little. I even played some when I was about ten. I did all my work quickly, and then I would turn to making my doll. I would sweep the house, pick over the beans, put them up to cook, warm the water, and bring some water up from the well; by then I could carry some water and Mama's well was near the house. When I had done all of that I would hurry up to make my doll, hurry to play. Then I would get careful again when I thought it was time for Mama to get back. I would see if the beans were cooking well; I put a wooden spoon into the pot to make sure that the water didn't boil over. I didn't get too lost in my play anymore because I was afraid of getting whipped. Mama was very strict. I would listen carefully; I always could hear when she came because Papa had a horse. When I heard them coming I would hurry to hide my dolls. That was my work when I was growing up.

Mama taught me. "See that your beans cook well," she would say. "Don't let the water run over. If it runs over you'll see the whip!"

"Yes, Mama," I answered softly.

"If the bean broth is clear like water that means that it ran over!"

"Yes."

I said yes, but I played. I got plenty of spankings. If something wasn't done right, if we forgot something because of our play, we'd get it. We were afraid. That's why I never took the spoon out of the bean pot. Of course, I also watched how Mama did things. She never said, "This is how you have to do it," but rather, "Watch your beans, don't let the water run over. If it runs over the broth will taste like water."

"Yes," I would answer. I made good beans, with good, thick broth. Then I wouldn't get scolded. But if the water ran over I got a scolding.

Mama says that when we were very little we lived in a place that didn't have any water nearby. One day after she went off with Papa to get some it began to pour. We tried to catch all we could as it fell from the roof, and when they got back all the storage jugs were filled. They hadn't bothered to go on to the river. "Let's see if the girls catch any, or if the cistern fills at all," they said. When they saw that we had filled all the storage jugs and even the cistern I remember that Mama said, "Sir, the girls have water." "Perhaps they know how to think now," said Papa. We had been running around in the water, filling all the jugs and emptying them into the cistern, until finally there was no place left to store the water. It had rained very hard. According to Mama we were very intelligent when we were growing up.

I was about eight when I began to make tortillas. Sometimes when she and Papa went to town she would leave the dough on the grinding table, and, naughty me, I would begin to make tortillas. I didn't want to eat the tortillas she had left, I wanted to eat my own. Sometimes she scolded me because I would invite my playmates to eat some. One time I broke her comal and she scolded me. And she scolded me for inviting my friends to eat. "Why do you play with the dough? I have to make the tortillas when I get home." "Yes," I would say, but I wanted to eat my own tortillas rather than hers.

Then I became a bit more prudent and stopped inviting my friends, but I still made tortillas for myself, perhaps because I was so capricious. Sometimes my tortillas came out very thick.

"What beautiful tortillas you have! You've been playing with the dough again." I hid my head in shame; I didn't answer properly because I was afraid. But I never stopped playing with the dough; I just became more careful. I would take off a little piece, rearrange the mound so it wouldn't show, and hide my little ball of dough.

"You've been playing with the dough. I didn't leave so little."

"No," I would say.

"You played with it. You are shameless."

I hung my head. But if she and Papa got home late then she didn't say anything because by then her dough would have turned sour.

By the time I was about nine I could make good tortillas, and Papa ate them. Mama taught me. She said, "Grind the dough well, make the tortillas well." That's how we learned. If the tortillas didn't come out right, she would roll half-baked tortillas right off the comal around on our palms. We shrieked with pain. Our palms would get all red. I was about nine or ten when she did that. "Why did your tortillas come out ugly?" she would ask. She really expected me to learn by then, to do them well. By the time I was eleven I was making them so well that we could give them to our workers.

When I first learned to turn the tortillas over on the griddle I used to burn myself. I would try to do it with just my finger tips. "This is how you have to turn them, not just with your finger tips," Mama said. Little by little I learned until I could use my whole hand. I was also afraid of laying them on the griddle. "I'm going to burn the hair on my arm," I would say. [Sometimes the flames leap up over the edge of the griddle.] Sometimes I placed the tortilla well, but sometimes it was all creased and sometimes it fell onto the ashes. Sometimes I put it too far to the edge of the griddle and it would double over. Then little by little I lost my fear of the fire. I also learned to care for the fire under the griddle. Mama showed me how.

We also went to get wood and to care for the animals. We would gather up the cut wood and carry it home. Once I got strong I wanted to carry a lot, not just a little bit. I also liked to carry a lot of water; I was only eleven when I began to use the big jug.[2] I wanted to carry the big one and let Mama carry my little one. "You'll suffer from carrying too much," she said, but she let me carry it. I was very naughty.

A Chamula woman remembered:

When I was about three or four my parents got me a little gourd to carry, and also a doll, one of those sold in San Cristobal. I was very happy with my doll. I carried her everywhere, to the well atop my gourd or the tiny water jug they got me later, to the steambath; I even slept with her. When she cried, I would hug her. I was happy with my doll.

Sometimes we played with mud. We would grind it and then pretend to make tortillas, as though we were big girls already. When my parents were busy we would leave and hide somewhere to make our tortillas. When our mother saw us she would scold us, saying that if we made mud tortillas we would never learn to make real ones. When she scolded us we would run away and look for another place to hide where we could make our tortillas.

When I was bigger my older brother showed me how to herd the sheep. I was afraid; the forest frightened me. There was one ram that liked to get away; when I discovered he was gone I would cry. The other children teased me, saying that it was lost forever, that a coyote would eat it. I was very worried. But they only teased me because they had seen that it was right there. As soon as I saw it I felt better.

My older brother told me that I shouldn't lose track of the sheep but I always lost them. They would get into someone's cornfield, and I wouldn't realize it until someone came to tell me. The owners of the cornfield would scold me. To keep the sheep from getting away while I played, I would hobble them.

Sometimes a ewe wandered into the forest. I searched and searched, but I was afraid to go very far; sometimes I wouldn't find her until the next day. When I lost an animal I didn't come into the house; I would sleep in the steambath, afraid of a scolding. But even though I got scolded, I never did get beaten. My parents would say, "You're to blame for losing the ewe. Maybe you'll find it tomorrow." They told me to get up very early to look for it.

When the sheep got into a cornfield my parents would have to pay for the damage; they said that perhaps it would be better if I didn't herd any more sheep. I thought, "O.K., let my older brother do it." But when he got bigger I had to go out with the sheep again. I was very careful at first, but after the first two or three days the sheep would get lost again.

Another time I had a ram that butted a lot and liked to go far afield looking for ewes. Then I would find some other children to help me bring it back. Even though I hobbled it, it would be off again pretty soon.

I never had more than four or five sheep at a time; we never had many. In the beginning, when I was just a little girl [perhaps six], I would go with my brothers. They would go off, leaving the sheep in my care, but I never paid attention. When they got back the sheep would be gone, and they would send me after them. I just pretended to search. When they saw that I hadn't found

---

[2] A large water jug weighs about 22 pounds empty and approximately 70 pounds when completely filled.

the sheep they threatened to tell our parents and sent me off to look for them again. When my brothers saw that I still hadn't found them they would get very angry and hit me. Then I would cry.

It was even worse when I felt sleepy. When I got home I would corral the sheep I had brought and I would go back to find the rest. Sometimes it would turn dark while I was out searching, and my parents would scold me for being out at night. Then I had to confess, and they would threaten to spy on me the next day to see if I really did watch the sheep or if I just played.

But when I got bigger [perhaps twelve] I became more responsible and began to teach my younger brothers. Once they learned to watch the sheep, I stopped herding.

When I was little and went out with the sheep my mother gave me some wool to spin but I never finished it. There was another girl there who was bigger and who played all day. She would begin to do her spinning only when she saw the sun going down. Since she didn't have time to finish her work she would hide it somewhere, but she never found it again. She advised me to do the same, but I was afraid of a scolding so I never did. She played all day or slept. She would come to the field and go right to sleep. When it was time to move the sheep we would have to wake her.

When I got home in the evening my mother would check on my work; since I had hardly done anything she would scold me, saying that all I had done was play. When we got still bigger we stopped playing; by then we were ashamed.

When I was a little girl [perhaps seven], my older brothers made me go with them to get firewood. They lassoed me and practically dragged me after them. One time they gave me a lot of wood to carry; it was too heavy and I fell. They said they made the bundle so heavy because I was very lazy. I nearly broke my legs. I cried a lot, I was frightened, but they made me go with them. When my mother didn't go for wood I didn't want to go either; I only was happy when I went with her. I didn't like the way my brothers treated me.

When I was still bigger my brothers began to tell me to cut the wood myself. Since I didn't know how I just cut my legs and began to howl. My brothers said I wasn't good for anything; I limped all the way home. But my brothers got a bad scolding for making me cut the wood instead of doing it themselves. I was also able to get back at my brothers by breaking their playthings. I began to handle the wood well when I was perhaps eleven years old. But I never did have to chop it with an axe because I had brothers; I only had to use a machete.

Sometimes we had to sell firewood. I went with my mother, carrying my little load of wood, and sometimes I cried because I got so tired. But that was a long time ago.

I was very little when I first learned to make tortillas and my tortillas were very, very little. First I made them on a leaf. Then my mother told me to make them in my hands; she said I had to learn, no matter what. By the time I was seven I knew how to make them, but it wasn't easy to learn. At first they came out very thick. When I finally got one made I put it on the griddle and sometimes it got stuck there; then I might burn my hand. My mother told me to keep an eye on the tortillas. Sometimes my mother would scold me when they didn't turn out right; she said it was my obligation as a woman to make them right. She said that because I like to play with mud I couldn't make real ones.

When I began to grind the corn I also hurt my fingers; we didn't have a hand mill then, just a stone *metate*. My brothers had to learn to grind corn, too. Those who knew how to grind could make their own *pozol* [uncooked corn gruel]; the others didn't get any. So I learned to grind corn.

When I was little I didn't know how much corn would fit into a cooking pot. Sometimes I put in too much and the [clay] pot would burst. Sometimes I put in too much lime, other times not enough. I also learned how to make the beans and the vegetables. At first everything came out raw. I got scolded a lot because my playing made me forget everything else, forget that others were hungry. But there are other mothers who scold their daughters much more and hit them or pull their hair. I wasn't treated very badly. It's true that if we had all been daughters my father would have bothered us a lot, but we were almost all boys.[3]

I began to accompany my mother to the well when I was a little girl, carrying my play gourd, and then a tiny water jug. Little by little the jugs got bigger until, when I was about thirteen, but not really very strong yet, I said to my mother one day that I wanted to take a full sized jug to the well. She let me, but my jug never got back to the house; it broke on the way. Then I got a real scolding. Little by little I got stronger until I really was able to carry a full-sized jug.

By the time I was about eleven I could make tortillas well, and soon after I could cook and do all the other housework. When my parents had to go somewhere they would find that I had taken care of all the chores. Little by little I learned.

Parents do not hold a rigid timetable or standard against which to measure their children's growth; rather, they accept the pattern and rate of their development, expecting considerable variation from one child to another. However, by the age of ten or eleven a child is expected to know, in more than a rudimentary fashion, almost everything he will need to know as an adult, except (for girls) to weave or (for some boys) to play a musical instrument. Adolescent girls are taught to weave in much the same fashion as they were taught all the other skills when they were younger. A Chamula woman remembered:

What was hard for me to learn was to weave. When I was little my mother gave me some wool to spin, but I was no good at it. When I went with her to the well I would find some wool along the path and try to turn it into thread; it didn't matter what color it was, I'd try to spin it all together. When I finally could do it a little I asked my parents to get me a spindle.

Then I tried to weave my scraps into something because my mother had told me that it was time for me to begin to learn my work; it came out completely shapeless. When my mother saw that I finally could make something she told me that it was time for me to make a blouse. She prepared the loom; I was very scared that it would come out wrong and wove with a lot of fear. Then my mother told me to make myself a little shawl, that she would show me how. I worked on it for a long time but I couldn't finish it; my mother had to finish it for me. My shawl ended up with lots of threads and almost without any form. It was hard for me to learn; I was more interested in playing. My mother would say to me, "Hurry up! If not, you'll never learn to work." Or, "Do it right. If you can't get it into your head, we'll have to punish your hands and slap them with the spindle." And sometimes she would grab my hands and slap them with the spindle until I shrieked. It was very hard for me to learn.

When my mother saw that I was doing a little better, she told me to make a tortilla bag, and I was very pleased. But she still had to set everything up. As she threaded the loom she showed me what to do. I began very enthusiastically, but by the end I had lost interest and didn't finish. I was really no good at those things. When my mother explained how I should make the bag I would begin to cry. Sometimes I would get so angry I wanted to rip my weaving apart with a knife or something sharp. My sister-in-law would say, "It's a difficult thing to learn, but set your mind to it. You'll learn." I suffered a great deal. I already

---

[3] The only other girl in the family is about eleven years younger.

knew a little, but I felt that I wasn't capable of learning. That's why I said it was better to rip it up. I never did, but my mother had to finish my work for me.

Then she told me to felt the wool. I spent a long time, trying and trying to shrink it, but it was no use; my mother had to do it. My mother had shown me how, but I thought I would never learn. She told me not to lose patience, that I would learn little by little.

Then she told me to make myself another blouse. It was the same thing all over again; she had to finish it. As soon as she finished she told me to make a skirt; that's a big job. I began it, and this time I finished it, but it was very hard. That was the first piece I was able to finish. The skirt was so wide I could hardly reach the sides of the loom. It took me a long time but this time I was able to finish it.

A long time passed, and then I began to make my big shawl. By then I was a better worker, but I had the same troubles as with my skirt. Again, I was able to finish it by myself, and my mother was pleased. She told me I had almost learned how to weave and that I was still young to do so well. I was perhaps ten or eleven years old then.

Then they told me to make a very heavy shawl, to begin with the edge. But because that's much harder than an ordinary piece of weaving, I trembled as I worked; I was afraid that it would turn out wrong. First my mother told me how to do it, then she went to the well. When she returned she asked me if I had finished it, but I said I couldn't figure out how to do it, that everything was all mixed up. She said, "I left you a sample and you spoiled it all." Then she made me take it apart and there I was, working away at undoing what I had done. Finally I was able to finish it.

When she began to show me how to prepare the looms a new era of suffering began. Again I felt that I would never learn, that I would never be able to make a skirt for myself. But my mother said that I had to learn and she showed me how; it seemed almost impossible to do.

After all of that my mother said that the least I could do was to make a blouse for myself. I don't know how old I was then, but I do know that I trembeld with fear because my mother scolded me; she said that she wasn't going to be around to make my clothing for me all the rest of my life. She told me what I had to do, that I couldn't keep on playing forever, that this was a woman's work. Little by little, I learned, until I could finally make myself a blouse and everything else.

I was about sixteen when I finally lost my fear of weaving. Now it's not so hard, and I like to work. But even then if I stop weaving for a long time I forget a bit. If I study a piece of clothing I can see how it was made and remember how to do it. I can even help with my father's clothing now. I don't cry any more but I still have to ask my mother for help; I still have trouble splicing in the thread.

When I first began to weave, my mother and I went to visit the Virgin who lives in our town. My mother said we shouldn't eat beforehand. We offered some little candles and asked the Virgin to put the art of weaving into my heart. My mother also said we had to speak with God. She said that when she had been a girl they had done the same with her, that they had come to ask the Virgin to light her way and make her learning easier. I said everything my mother told me to say. I went to church two or three times, as everyone should who wants to learn. We spoke to our Mother, the Mother of the Heavens, the Mother of God. Women who know more about these things say that we should take a sample of our weaving to the Virgin to show her how stupid we are and that we should leave this sample at her feet. But I only gave her my few little candles.

A woman from Chenalho remembered:

When I was about fifteen I began to use the spindle. My mother taught me. I watched how she did it and she said to me, "Prepare your thread, spin it. Go find some thread. You have to make your napkin; you have to make your shawl." Since my aunt still lived with us then, she showed me how to weave; my mother just taught me how to spin. "Do it this way," my mother would say, "Don't make it too soft or too hard." When my spindle didn't turn right she would hit me with it. It was hard to make thread; in those days we had to spin it ourselves, but now we can buy it all ready for the loom. My mother would say, "Where did you come from, woman, that you don't know how to handle your spindle? Women have to learn. You'll probably have a strict mother-in-law who knows how to weave very well, and she'll scold you. She'll hit you on your head with the spindle and the whorl if you don't know how to use them. That's the only way you'll ever learn to weave."

When I learned how to weave I got hit less because it was my aunt who taught me. "Do it this way. Brocade like this. It's not necessary to scold if you want to learn." My aunt was good to me. "Some people say it's necessary to hit with the weaving instruments, but it's not if we really want to learn." It seemed that I didn't have any eyes with which to see, with which to count the threads, but she was very patient. "Do it this way," she would say. I cried a lot but, little by little, God helped me and I learned.

My aunt would begin by showing me. Then she would say, "Go on. Look at what I am doing. You have to leave a thread in the middle; you have to grab one; you have to grab three. It depends on the design." It was very hard to brocade. But I finished my shawl in just two or three months, and it didn't come out too badly either. Then I began copying other kinds of clothing, blouses, and other things. Then nobody showed me; I just followed a model.

My mother sent me to the church to pray to the Virgins. "Go to them. Cry to them that you want to learn. You have to beg them, for brocading belongs to the Virgins."

"Yes," I said, and went to speak to them. I told them all that was in my heart.

Boys who learn to play musical instruments seem to have a much easier time of it, perhaps because such knowledge is considered esoteric, not required of all. Some are self-taught. After purchasing an instrument the learners will watch and then figure out for themselves the fingerings needed for a given piece; they then repeat them endlessly until they have mastered them and the playing has become almost automatic. Others receive more direct instruction from someone who already knows how to play, but they, too, rely primarily upon observation and imitation for learning. Few musicians, especially those who play the stringed and wind instruments, know the entire tribal repertoire.

While boys can earn money with their farming skills, girls have fewer opportunities for economic independence. Women in almost all the tribes have a few chickens and earn small sums from the sale of birds and eggs, but they rarely acquire chickens of their own until they have moved away from both parents and in-laws. Amatenangueras are encouraged toward independent earnings from middle childhood through the sale of their pottery; married Chamula and Zinacantecan women (but not their unmarried daughters) often own sheep whose wool they either sell or use for their own weaving. A handful of women in most tribes and a larger proportion of Chamulas sell their weaving and sometimes their spinning.

Boy and father drumming at a fiesta, Chenalho.

It is only in these last activities that adolescent girls may earn independently, but few do. Rather, parents are expected to meet all the financial needs of their daughters, including occasional jewelry. Most girls marry during the early or middle teens (indeed, many learn to weave or make pottery from their mothers-in-law rather than from their own mothers), after which their young husbands are expected to adorn them a bit more than their fathers did. It is only after they are established in homes of their own that they begin to earn for themselves. Of course, the few girls who have become teachers break with this and many other patterns, for they move away and begin to earn independently during the later teens, marry some years later, and then often marry Indian teachers from other tribes.

Young children are allowed to sleep during the day and often are held in the arms or tied onto someone's back to help them nap. They are allowed to sleep as late as they wish in the mornings. As they grow into working age first daytime napping is discouraged and then they are prodded into awakening earlier. Women generally get up well before dawn and long before their husbands, to relight the fire and begin making tortillas. An ideal girl begins to keep her mother's hours and help with the early morning chores by about the age of ten or eleven. Others expect their daughters to awaken before their mothers, as training for becoming good wives. However, many parents let their children sleep later. Boys of about ten may be sent to guard the ripening corn from marauding animals early in the morning; this, however, is only a seasonal chore. Many girls do not learn to awaken before dawn until they have married, many boys until they have begun to assume a man's economic responsibilities.

Outright disobedience is not tolerated once a child is believed to "understand," and the punishments may be quite severe. One or two generations ago children were hung over the smoking fire, sometimes head down, or were made to breathe the smoke of burning chiles. Food, or at least salt, might be denied them, or the mouth might be rubbed with chile. Such punishments appear to be rare now. Children are scolded frequently, and often spanked, sometimes with a leather strap or switch, but they are usually struck only once or twice, not repeatedly. Or a child may be assigned the tasks he likes least. A common punishment for a particularly recalcitrant child in Oxchuc and Chanal is to tie him by his hands to a stake near the house; he will be freed at night to sleep, but may be retied the next day, until his anger has passed and he has submitted to the parental will. Yet such a child will not be denied more than one meal a day. It is also expected that in the course of scolding or punishing parents explain to him what he did wrong. The denial of food is considered the worst of all punishments; many adults claim to have never been denied their food as children.

Fathers are expected to be stricter than mothers, and to demand a quieter house; children should be more fearful of their fathers. Yet it is often the women who appear to be more impatient and stricter, perhaps because they have fewer outlets for their hostilities than do the men.[4] It is believed that if a child is not scolded and otherwise punished into working and into obedience he will grow up to be rude, playful, disobedient, and a drunkard. Some feel that a woman has the right to order her children about since she suffered so much during their birth. Others feel that too much scolding saddens a child profoundly and that it should be avoided as much as possible.

By about the age of eleven or twelve a girl should be able to take full responsibility for running a household, although she is not expected to weave or embroider yet. All thoughts of play should have been left behind. In most tribes she is considered marriageable and will, in all likelihood, be married within the next few years. Girls are generally about twelve or fourteen when they first begin to weave, and are not expected to master all the skills until about the age of sixteen, often after marriage.

A boy of about twelve should also have become a good worker, although he is not expected to do as much as a man until he has reached full physical maturity and strength at about twenty. While he spends a number of years working hard and saving a bit of money, he does not seriously consider finding a wife until the later teens, when he can assume a fully adult stance.

Although parents rarely praise, and then only as a child begins to learn a new skill, they come to rely more and more on their child's work and to appreciate its genuine contribution to the household economy. In turn, the child is expected

---

[4] Women, unlike men, should not get drunk, and relatively few do. Men tend to drink far more. It is only when very drunk, when a person has lost all self-control, that outward expressions of hostility, especially physical aggression, are pardonable.

to sense his parents' attitudes and to know that his work is appreciated. While scoldings are frequent, they are often no more than a word or phrase, often coupled with a short explanation or exhortation to behave correctly or more adultly; "lazy" is one of the strongest expletives. Or a child may overhear a parent reporting on his accomplishments to another adult. It is only when drunk that a parent may tell a child directly of his love for him.

In turn, children often do appear to know how their parents feel about them. In a relatively small community where people are highly dependent upon one another the ability to perceive and understand others is highly functional and likely to be well developed. So it is with most Highlanders, who are especially concerned with and usually quite accurate at reading another's intentions towards them. Women appear to be even more perceptive and knowledgeable about the attitudes and feelings of others than are men.

There is one role which is exclusively children's: the performance of tasks which are outside the ken of proper adult behavior. Thus the woman who needs help in carrying water is far more likely to call upon her preteen son, even if he has to make several trips, than to ask her husband, at least if any neighbors are likely to see. Children are also sent on errands, especially to borrow or buy food from kin or neighbors, and at the same time to report home what they have seen. It is expected that in the process of running such errands children will learn something about money and the value of things. They are sent only as far as they can comfortably walk; for a six-year-old this probably means within a mile or two but older children may walk two or three hours in each direction to accomplish such a task.

EMOTIONAL EXPRESSION AND INTELLECTUAL DEVELOPMENT

The people tend to be quite direct and intense in their feelings, even though the expression of most emotions, especially hostility, may be discouraged and they may find it difficult to state explicitly what it is that they are feeling. One is not expected to alter one's behavior markedly in accord with the emotions; only young children commonly do so. Rather an older child or adult is expected to continue in the patterns of his work regardless of his mood.

In Oxchuc anger is felt in the head and face; "We would like to bite the person," said one informant. But love, sorrow, and fear are felt in the heart; then the fear may spread throughout the body. The common way to ask about another's mood or feelings among all the tribes is, in effect, "What does your heart say?" The usual reply is "Nothing" if a person is unaware of any strong mood; "Contented," at a moment of great joy; or "Sorrow."

Parents express deep sorrow and cry freely in front of their children. At such times, as at a death in the family, a child may try to comfort a parent, talking to him, even trying to dry his eyes. And the parents, in turn, are deeply moved. The people are aware of various forms of loving and differentiate the love of a child from that of a sibling, parent, or spouse. However, the effort is made to continue the correct form of behavior at all times. Even when older children are very angry with a parent they rarely drop the correct and very respectful forms of address.

Children are generally expected to be seen but not heard in or near the home. The only exception is for the very young, those who are "too young to understand." Babies are allowed to babble and young children to speak as loudly as they wish. Crying is discouraged and the baby is comforted as quickly as possible. Temper tantrums are frequent at about two years of age, as children are expected to begin to learn correct behavior and the passive acceptance of all events. Some parents consider tantrums a symptom of stomach illness brought on by the denial of some requested food, others consider them reactions to any type of denial or frustration, to jealousy over a yet unborn child, or to sibling rivalry. Others consider tantrums merely willful behavior.

If an angry child is still nursing, his mother may first attempt to give him her breast as a pacifier, possibly to be thanked with a bite. She may respond by hitting him as she probably would with an already weaned child. Either this quiets him, "because of the pain of the spank," or he may throw himself to the ground. Only drunks or toddlers in the height of tantrums are likely to do this, for lying (even sitting) directly on the ground is generally taboo. It is expected that the tantrum will soon pass and that the child will fall asleep to awaken refreshed and the anger forgotten.

Frequent tantrums are cured by Baptism, which forces the devil away, or, if the child has already been baptized, by prayers in the church. A mother may threaten to have her child given an injection, or she may pick at his head while he is in full tantrum until he bleeds, thus releasing the bile which caused the anger and ending the tantrum. Other mothers think of their furious children as overheated and bathe them in cold water. When all else fails a female curer is called upon to perform the appropriate ceremonies and thus end the tantrums. These spells, however, are seldom as full-blown or as lengthy as those common in the United States, for they are avoided whenever possible; indeed, that which is labeled a tantrum by the Highlanders we would be more likely to consider merely a passing episode of rather mild frustration.

Anger in older children or adults is believed to form a tumor in the heart which may be relieved by an herb (fennel) tea. It is recognized, at least by women, that parents sometimes vent their own frustrations on their children, as do drunks on any member of the family who may be present. Children's behavior is sometimes recognized to reflect parental moods or the thwarting of their wishes.

Children are brought up to be very fearful of anyone other than a member of the immediate family. When a stranger enters the house, even on a formal visit, a young child may be told over and over again that the person has come to rob or to give him an injection. The adults do this playfully while cuddling the child against the implied danger, and continue to do so until the child shrinks in fear and begins to cry. Then they soothe him, assuring him that within the security of the family he is safe. One of the signs of maturity is when children, especially boys, are ready to brave the implied dangers and deal with outsiders. Children also come to fear the dark, bodies of water, being left alone, new and strange objects and events, most animals, fighting or bickering, and threats of supernatural evil figures, such as the *pukuj* (devil) or, more recently, with the coming of modern medicine, being injected. For instance, they may be told that the max (a representation of the pukuj) will eat them if they do not behave themselves. Many of these fears continue throughout life.

Children past the toddling stage are often expected to be jealous of their younger siblings, although the reverse is less expected and some informants negate any such jealousies. Neither should toddlers be expected to express jealousy of the newborn, although they may resent his being breastfed. However, several informants report that a child may throw a temper tantrum at the sight of any pregnant woman, not necessarily even one he has ever known before. Vogt (1969) suggests that the resentments of younger boys against their older brothers remains dormant throughout childhood, to be felt later as brothers compete for the limited land of their father. A strong senior-junior principle is built into all relationships, social and ceremonial; the senior is always in a position of authority while the junior must obey and serve him.

Children are expected to be jealous of one another's toys. They are considered the owners of toys given to them or that they have made, but are encouraged to share and play with them together, without friction. This seldom seems to be a serious problem. But the jealousy over toys, mild as it may be, is merely the precursor of adult jealousy over the possessions of others, with neighbors continually casting backward glances to see what others have acquired. Cornfields are mentally measured and counted; in herding tribes the same happens with the sheep and cattle, the clothing one wears to work or the fiestas is evaluated, one's house is appraised, and the acquisition of anything as novel as a radio or phonograph is avidly gossiped about. Some people state that they fear that they will go hungry when another has so much more than they. Ideally a man returns his accumulated wealth to the community by taking on a religious cargo to sponsor a fiesta; many men of "wealth" do this. For all people there is the danger that unless the acquisition of wealth is the result of clear and acceptable outside sources of income, such as money accumulated at a coffee plantation, accusations of witchcraft may follow; this is especially true at times of crisis. In Oxchuc, where belief in witchcraft is dying out, cases of theft and of theft accompanied by murder are not unheard of, although witchcraft is now seldom mentioned as the motive.

Although each object within the home may have its owner, it is expected that any member of the family should have access to it. Sharing is strongly encouraged and learned early so that children barely out of the toddling stage may be seen in the market sharing a piece of bread or some other goody with one another. According to one informant, sharing within the family is merely the natural way of behaving.

At the same time, children are taught from the time they begin to toddle not to touch things which do not belong to the family; even a baby who touches something belonging to an outsider is said to be robbing it. It is for such robberies that older children may receive the strongest of punishments. In Oxchuc this is the time when a child may be bound to a pole for three or four days and denied food.

A Chamula boy of about twelve was alleged to have been severely flogged by the tribal authorities several years ago after being jailed for a couple of days for stealing money from neighbors' houses; he then robbed again and fled the community, never to return. His father was subsequently accused of witchcraft by many of the neighbors. These rumors continued long after he had repaid all of the boy's debts.

Quarreling among siblings is discouraged, although verbal aggression is generally less censured than physical aggression. Children who bite or hit one another may find themselves spanked in return. A good child is always humble, accepting whatever the gods have in store for him, although he may tattle on an older sibling in self-defense. Parents generally favor their younger children under such circumstances and are more prone to punish the older ones. Some children learn to play one parent off against the other.

Physical aggression against the parents is completely taboo once it is recognized; young children may be merely ridiculed or told not to hit their parents, but older ones may be severely punished. Verbal aggression toward parents is less serious and sometimes merely ignored. Thus a child may call his mother a whore in a fit of anger and elicit little or no response from her. However, in adolescence, as the struggle for independence gains ascendancy, youngsters may fight more openly with their parents, even striking them; in most cases, the struggle for independence and adulthood remains more covert. The young couple marries in the girl's home but after a while moves to the boy's, supposedly to remain there for several years. Although married and perhaps even a father, a boy continues under the domination of his father; the girl is virtually a servant to her mother-in-law. While the boy may have already become a more than adequate farmer, the girl may still have to master the techniques of weaving or pottery making. Although the basic struggle for independence is usually between the boy and his father, it is some disagreement between the girl and her mother-in-law which is most often seized upon as the excuse to set up an independent household, often only a few feet away from the father's.

Once the couple achieves independence the most common causes of domestic fights are accusations that the woman has denied adequate food to her husband, that the man has struck his wife whether sober or drunk (and supposedly unaware of his behavior), laziness on the part of either, or infidelity.

Idle boasting is also discouraged, unless a person states an accepted truth about his skills. Gossiping, as long as it proves accurate or cannot be disproven, is encouraged, but lying is not. To discourage boasting and lying parents are apt to tease their children, returning verbal aggression in kind.

Although anger is recognized, it is often considered dangerous, a possible invitation to the gods to visit illness or other tragedy upon the family. Contentment, fear, and sorrow are about the only emotions which are given legitimate expression. Happiness is having enough food to eat, including enough protein; it is having enough money to eat well and to dress well in the fiestas; it is having the land and domestic animals which allow for such wealth. It also means having a spouse who is a hard worker, helpful, and slow to anger, and having many children of both sexes; and, lastly, being able to serve the community either through political or religious offices, held directly by the men but with the considerable assistance of their wives. For children it means having warm, patient, and loving parents, enough food to eat, enough clothing to keep warm, and a rich play life with several playmates and a few toys. For school children it also means doing well at one's studies, having a good teacher, and getting along well with one's classmates.

Sorrow comes not only from the death of a beloved member of the family or from loneliness. It is also felt to be the reverse of happiness. Thus going hungry or poorly clothed, living with angry or hostile people, or any major frustration, are all felt to cause much sorrow.

Over one hundred children were asked in a pilot study for the reading test (see Chapter 5) about a boy who, in reaching for some fruit, fell off the branch of a tree and hurt himself. In responding to a question about how the boy felt after his fall, they were given a choice of angry, sad, or happy; all who responded stated that he felt sad.

To be able to deal with ladinos effectively and in Spanish, and to defend one's position, are sources of considerable pride and pleasure; to be defenseless before ladinos and dependent upon their (often questionable) honesty is a source of great shame and sorrow.

Individual differences among children are readily recognized. Parents feel no sense of responsibility for a child's basic character, although they do feel considerable responsibility for training him in the correct ways of behaving and working. As with emotions, one's basic character structure is of less importance than one's day-to-day behavior. That one fulfills all of his obligations and is, above all, a hard worker (despite the mood of the minute) is what matters. With little or no sense of responsibility invested in a child's basic character, parents are easily able to accept differences in personality and in modes of responding. Yet, while noting these differences, they tend to ignore them as they train their children, unless such differences speed up the training. The child who likes to ape his elders is generally more appreciated than the one who resists maturity; the former is "good," the latter playful, mischievous, lazy, or "bad."

Little is done to foster the development of fantasy in children. As long as they work well, whether or not they fantasize is of relatively little importance. Yet dreams do play a large part in children's development. Dream symbolism has been codified and dreams are systematically analyzed. For the most part the dream states a present or future fact, often in reverse. Thus, to dream of someone becoming ill may be to wish him good health, but to dream of him well may predict his illness, even death. In addition to their predictive powers, dreams may identify a person's animal soul-companion to him. It is only through one's own dream, never through the wishes or dreams of the parents, that a person can know his soul or possible ability to heal, to become a curer.

The ability to memorize is more readily recognized than the ability to fantasize. A father is expected to tell his son the names and uses of all the plants; ideally the boy should remember after only one hearing. The same is true of girls, who learn primarily from their mothers. Memorization, an essential part of school life as much as at home, is considered a natural development, one not requiring training. The child who is serious will remember; the playful one will forget. Other lore which should be memorized, such as common prayers, is learned through accompanying one's parents and listening to them year after year until the child, too, knows the litany. Any part dramatic play may have in the mastery of these prayers is not recognized.

The major stories and myths are learned and handed down from one generation to another; the children hear them over and over again and are instructed in their meanings. The stories are told and gossip exchanged at the dawn or evening meals or whenever the family gathers around the hearth. The little children nestle up against their parents or an older relative, often nodding with sleep, the older ones sit listening, often intently. Yet the children are free to leave the group if they wish, and often do so once their attention has wandered.

Religion cannot be separated from any other aspect of living; it permeates all of life. Children begin imitating the religious ceremonies almost as soon as they begin dramatic play shortly after the toddler stage. They imitate their parents at prayer, the curing ceremonies, and the major ceremonies which take place in the tribal center. They learn their prayers by listening to their parents over and over again and later begin to mouth the words after them. There is no pressure for them to pray on their own until the teen years, by which time they should have learned at least the rudimentary prayers well. Most never learn the others, so that even ceremonial leaders often call on a particularly knowledgeable person to help with the special prayers of a major ceremony. Personal prayers are often improvised, following the general style and format appropriate to the occasion.

Kinship terms, correct forms of address, and much of the highly formal etiquette which marks all social exchanges except those within the immediate family are learned in much the same way as other skills, by observation and imitation. Godparents do not receive the same importance as in the ladino culture. In Chamula, and to a lesser extent in other municipios, grandparents, uncles, or aunts are the ones most often called upon to sponsor a child for Baptism, thus negating the function of *compradasco* for extending family ties to unrelated persons.

Children are expected to be respectful of their elders, including their older siblings. There are separate terms for older brother, older sister, and younger sibling in all the tribes; the specific forms vary somewhat from one tribe to another. Older siblings are expected to stand as parent surrogates, especially in the absence of the parent of the same sex; younger siblings are expected to defer to them as though they were almost parents. In actual life sibling rivalries often override these considerations; younger siblings express their anger at older ones far more freely than they express anger at their parents. Although hitting is generally censured, hitting an older sibling is not as serious as hitting a parent. Boys are especially likely to feel jealousy as they vie for the father's approval and a major share of his lands. Where land is still available these rivalries may not be felt as intensely as in Chamula and Zinacantan where it is very scarce.

Since most tribal affairs, including the dispensing of justice, are carried out on the *cabildo* (town hall) porch, all are free to watch. Trials are held in public and a crowd, adults and children alike, usually gathers to hear both sides of the dispute

Child max, *Chamula.*

discussed, often simultaneously, by the litigants and their helpers. A solution is then sought by the town officials; it serves more to resolve the difficulty and restore harmony to the community than to invoke abstract standards of justice. A group of children, especially boys, is often seen intensely observing the process of governing.

In one trial in Chamula, where a man was accused of theft, he was ordered to pay, on the spot, the approximate value of the stolen goods; the accuser was told to be more careful of her property in the future; both were then fined by the court, told to resolve their difficulties, and never to fight again. Somewhat mollified, each having saved face and seen the other scolded and fined, they left the scene of the trial, probably resolving to avoid disputes of this kind in the future.

Men, especially young men who have acquired a reputation as trouble makers, are often pressed into government service for a year during which time it is hoped that they will learn correct behavior, and during which time they will suffer the privations of being able to carry on almost no gainful work; those occupying the lower positions of government usually leave office heavily in debt but hopefully enriched in the knowledge that they have served their community, one of the idealized values of all the tribes.

The learning of Spanish is considered desirable by all the people, as much for women as for men. Yet Spanish is rarely spoken within the home. Children learn the language primarily in school, although children who work for ladinos, primarily as servants, generally learn at least the rudiments of the language on the job. This is especially true for boys from Chamula and Zinacantan and girls from Chenalho, Mitontik, and Oxchuc, who most often fulfill such jobs. A rudimentary form of arithmetic, especially counting and making change up to about 5 pesos, is more often learned at the market. Children may begin to count in their mother tongue at about the age of six, at about the same time they have mastered conservation of numbers, but it appears that some achieve conservation without ever learning to count accurately.[5] Almost all remain dependent upon ladinos to furnish them with correct change when making a major purchase (such as the specific combination of many candles of different sizes and prices needed for a major curing ceremony) because they lack the ability to check on the accuracy of the money returned to them. (In the schools arithmetic is taught in a systematic fashion, largely in Spanish, although the numbers may be labeled in both languages. There is relatively little effort made to translate school arithmetic into its applications in the marketplace or elsewhere.) Other uses for numbers within the traditional society are even more limited. Workers must sometimes be paid for their help in farm work or house building, food and cloth measured, threads counted for brocading, ceremonial meals occasionally supplied, and, for those living near a brickworks or carpentry shop, building material occasionally purchased. But the major use of money and of counting outside the marketplace is in weddings, where many gifts must be given and a bride-price paid; all of this must be returned in the case of a divorce, so accounts are kept, often mentally, and strenuous efforts are made, especially by the girl's family, to keep a marriage going. The settling of such accounts after separation often involves considerable litigation.

Drawing is all but unknown by the children, except in Amatenango where girls begin early to practice the designs they will later paint on their pottery. Elsewhere girls rarely draw the highly stereotyped designs they brocade and embroider into their clothing. Men have even less need for drawing and rarely do so. However,

---

[5] Many informants state that some adult neighbors of theirs have never learned to count beyond two or three.

the few students who proceed through the more advanced elementary grades do receive some formal drawing lessons, often as a part of their science and social studies work.

Most Indians are quite accurate in recalling time and place within the recent past. But since many, except school children, cannot count accurately beyond five, counts get hazy after that. While parents may know the exact ages of their young children, they rarely know those of their older ones; nor, of course, do they know their own ages. Beyond the immediate past, time and distance tend to become confounded, so that that which happened long ago, especially before the lifetime of the teller, is often placed far away in space as well as in time (Gossen 1969).

The passage of the minutes and hours is rarely of import, but the day is divided into several parts, each with its appropriate tasks, according to the passage of the sun across the sky. Dawn, when the day begins and the people arise and eat a quick breakfast, often the remains of the evening meal, is followed by the morning, when the major, most taxing work of the day is undertaken. At about noon, when the sun is overhead, it is time for a short rest and a light meal, often merely some corn gruel or a couple of cold tortillas; some women, especially Chamulas, appear to skip this meal entirely. In the afternoon work resumes, but in the late afternoon, perhaps a couple of hours before dusk, most of the work of the day comes to an end and the women begin to prepare the evening meal, the major meal of the day, which is eaten at dusk. After nightfall the family sits chatting about the hearth for a while, the younger children are sent off to bed, and soon afterwards the rest of the family retires.

The days of the week are usually called by their Spanish names. In Oxchuc Saturday is a time for a few hamlet markets in which local produce is exchanged; usually one or two men have brought goods from San Cristobal for sale. Sunday is a time for larger markets in many of the tribal and other important trading centers. Ladino traders come to these markets, as well as Indians from several of the surrounding tribes, and there is much socialization.

Although some people still know and reckon by the Mayan calendar, most mark the passage of yearly time by the Spanish calendar, often using the names of the months as though they were seasons. Thus Chamulas may refer to February as the time of the planting, May as the time of weeding, and so on. The passage of the months is marked by changes in the shadows cast by trees and houses.

Distance is measured primarily by finger widths, hand spans, and arm spans, and children learn these measures largely by imitation. Greater distances are measured by paces and by the distance a mule train can cover in an hour. The latter is called a league and equals about 4 kilometers or roughly 2.5 miles. While some claim that a league is an absolute measure of distance, others appear to use the term loosely, speaking of longer and shorter leagues. Weather conditions also come into play, so that the same trail may be considered 4 leagues in the dry season but 6 during the heaviest of the rains. This is true for both Indians and ladinos. Land surfaces are measured by means of *tareas*, or *tablones*, the amount of land a man can clear or weed in a long morning's work, or according to the amount of land needed to plant one *litro* (20 metric liters) of corn. It is my impression that the tarea or tablon measures date from the time of Indian slavery, for a strong worker usually finishes two tareas in a day working on his own or when paid by the tarea by his neighbor. A young Oxchuquera who was freed from serfdom during her own childhood claimed that a good farmer could do five tareas in one day!

The most common measure of volume is the *porcelana*, which, apparently, is not perfectly standardized. The term *porcelana* refers to a small bowl of fairly standard shape, sometimes measuring less than a standard cup, sometimes about a third of a liter, and sometimes a whole liter. For this reason it is necessary for the purchaser to see the porcelana being used to measure his purchase and to estimate the relative size compared to others of its general dimensions. Largely through keen observation, children learn early to make these distinctions, although their accuracy is seldom called into question. Hot peppers, peanuts, and salt are some of the foods measured by the porcelana. Other common measures include the *quartita*, a small beer bottle which is used to measure liquids, gourds of various sizes used in the sale of chicha, liters, both liquid and dry, and the *quartilla* (.25 liter). Again, all of the measuring devices are made locally either of clay or of wood, with bottles reputed to contain a liter being used for the liquid measure. The largest measure of volume used is generally the *costal*, a large burlap bag which holds about 110 pounds of shelled corn. It is about the heaviest weight that a strong man can carry on his back with a tumpline. Other than the filled costal, weight is generally estimated by picking up an object, but is seldom labeled. Rather people evaluate whether or not they can carry it, and if not them, then whom. From the time they begin playing with the tumpline children learn to estimate weights.

There are two principal directions known, the East and the West, the places where the sun rises and sets; the North is called the side of the sun's path. There are few types of signaling done in these tight little mountain valleys, and there is apparently little need for it. Most pointing is done with the lower lip, which is raised over the upper lip as the chin is lifted in the indicated direction, or by extending the hand, all fingers held rigidly, in the proper direction; some tribes extend the arm and then rub the first three fingers in the desired direction. People may call to one another across a valley, often in a somewhat falsetto voice, almost chanting the call.

Weather is predicted by watching the formation and movement of the clouds. When the clouds cover the Sun, He cannot see the people, a fact which makes this a more perilous time than when He is shining. In order to assure adequate rain for the crops, pilgrimages are made to the church of Saint Thomas in Oxchuc every year at the beginning of the rainy season in May or June. The pilgrims include not only Tzeltales, but also Tojolabales, who come from as far away as a five days' march, carrying flutes and drums with them to accompany dancing for the saint and to lighten the weary hours along the trails. In Tzotzil communities prayers are offered to the crosses which mark the waterholes.

Children learn early, through hearing folktales repeated, that the Sun is the principal deity, often identified with a Christian God—Jesus Christ in Tzotzil communities, or Saint Thomas, the patron of Oxchuc, by most Tzeltales. Following ancient Mayan lore, the Moon is His mother. It was quite difficult for many of those Indians who heard about men landing on the Moon in 1969 to comprehend this feat, and many remained incredulous even when shown pictures from *Time* and

Life magazines. Some have blamed a subsequent influenza epidemic on the gringos for their rape of the Moon. Unlike the Sun and the Moon, the stars have relatively little importance in the religious lore.

The religious life of the family and the community is such that children participate from earliest infancy. A child attends ceremonies with his parents and may be a central figure in a curing ceremony. When a man is involved in a religious cargo he becomes sponsor or assumes other responsibilities for a fiesta, usually for a year (Vogt 1969). At such times he calls upon his extended family to help him fulfill the duties. Entire nuclear families respond to his request, often for several days at a time and several times during the year he is in office. This response often involves going to live in a special ceremonial house in the tribal center for a few days; parents appear to be accompanied by all their children, both those so young as to need considerable care and those old enough to help out on their own. It is not unusual to see children participate in these major ceremonies, either as helpers or merely by standing alongside their parents as the latter chant their prayers and fulfill their other obligations. As soon as a boy has learned to play a musical instrument with some skill, as some do by the age of ten, he may be called upon to help supply the music, like any adult musician.

The flora and fauna of the area offer children many opportunities for both play and learning. There are few poisonous plants in the Highlands, but many thorny ones. Children learn early which ones are good for playthings and which ones will hurt them. They regard the little animals of the forest as worthy targets for slingshots and traps, and once they have gotten hold of an animal they will often pull it apart while examining it. Smaller carcasses are generally fed to the family's dog or cat, but larger ones are either cooked over an open fire on the spot or brought home for a family meal. Most of the area is so overpopulated at this time, however, that meal-sized animals are rare indeed; some men go out to hunt rabbits or squirrel at night, but with little success. Only in the large, forested, and relatively uninhabited mountains is it possible sometimes to find a small deer, usually about two-feet high at the haunches. Children play with the family dogs, often making them the recipient of both their tender emotions and their hostilities. While a child may not caress anyone other than a baby, he is likely to caress the family dog.

Sex roles are highly prescribed, especially away from home. Girls learn a woman's work, largely the care of hearth and home and the clothing of the family. Boys learn a man's work, which is to provide food, shelter, and firewood for his family, and to participate in the religious and political governance of the town. Once children have reached the age at which they begin to learn to work, at about six or seven, they are discouraged from playing with members of the opposite sex, although they may work together in the fields or sit in the same classroom at school. In school it is rare to see a boy and girl of this age sharing the same desk, even though they are brother and sister. At home men tend to sit on one side of the hearth, often near the door, women on the other, near their cooking utensils. Interchanges between brother and sister at this age are almost exclusively verbal. In some tribes more effort is made than in others to chaperone adolescent girls in order to protect their virginity, the assumption being that without chaperonage girls would be attacked by the first unrelated man with whom they find themselves. As they learn to work they begin to assume more and more of the correct womanly modesty, feigning much shyness in public, especially in mixed company. They hide behind their shawls, often not uncovering their faces until some other activity, such as carrying, requires it. They are always careful to cover their faces when laughing or eating in school. Indeed, many a girl covers her face whenever a teacher calls on her, whether or not she mumbles an answer to his question. Boys, on the other hand, are expected to become braver and braver until they are valiant enough to talk to a stranger or to a new bride and in-laws.

Both sexes are supposed to keep their genitals well hidden when sitting. Men cover their trousers or shorts with their tunics when sitting or squatting. Women in Chamula and Zinacantan keep their legs tightly together when sitting, usually on the ground with their legs curled to one side. Sometimes they sit on their knees, but never squat in public. When they sit on a chair they usually cross their legs tightly at the ankles, with the legs held rigidly in front. In the other tribes women do squat in public, but they always tuck the back of their skirts tightly under the bent knees and then pull the front loosely over their legs to the ground. They may then double the front of the skirt under them to sit on it. Girls learn to sit this way shortly after they have been toilet-trained and as soon as the length of their skirts allows it. Those who sit with their legs separated in public are equally careful to cover their legs down to their ankles with their skirts. Only the genitals of toddlers not yet toilet-trained may be seen in public.

Parents are concerned that their children learn to reason for themselves, especially in the areas of farming and in understanding people. Although both sexes are concerned with both areas of reasoning, boys are particularly concerned with the former and girls with the latter. This desire to understand extends into all other areas of experience and is readily expressed by more advanced students despite the high degree of rote quality in the instruction they have experienced throughout their school years. Thus they want to understand Mexican history and the characters and roles of the men who influenced it, not merely to recite names and dates by rote. They want to understand the mathematical processes, not merely to calculate mechanically. The brighter students are often more curious, at least within the formal curriculum areas, than many of their teachers, who appear to have had their curiosity, at least in the academic areas, long since socialized out of them. Because of this desire to better understand the world, Protestantism, with its alternative explanations for many phenomena, has been able to catch hold in a number of communities, most notably in Oxchuc and its surrounding areas. People constantly seek explanations for that which they do not understand.

Recent work in Zinacantan has shown rather clearly that young children develop the intellectual structures described by Piaget at about the same rate as his Swiss subjects (Greenfield 1970). According to one anthropologist:

The Indians see education as a process that takes place from the time a child is born until he reaches the summit of his life. Then he begins to decline, his education ending with his death. Education (*nopesel* or *chanel*, Tzotzil; *no'pel*, Tzeltal) means to be conscious of the world where fate has placed him and shaped all the possibilities of his life. There is also a connotation of "becoming accustomed" in this concept of education, somewhat akin to the North American concept of training as opposed to problem solving. A situation is repeated as many times as necessary, until the child becomes accustomed and is able to perform as expected. Thus a child learns to stay at home uncomplainingly when his mother leaves the house for an hour or more. Thus an adult is accustomed to his daily tasks, although they once took him years to learn. A man learns to play the guitar by repeating the same song over and over again until his hand becomes accustomed to the movements and he need not think consciously of how to place it. The lengthy prayers are learned until they can be repeated faultlessly. A person explores his world and accustoms himself to his environment until he feels that he has learned all the traditions of his community. Having mastered his inheritance, he may feel that he has learned all, and begin to decline, to fade into death. But many an oldster feels that there is still more to learn, and so continues to have much curiosity about the world in which he finds himself and about the vague world beyond his own. This vague world beyond the immediate one may be either the mysterious world of the supernatural or the physical one rumored to exist beyond the furthest point to which any known person has traveled, such as the capital of Mexico or the United States beyond. The physical and supernatural worlds that exist beyond the known are not always differentiated.

The role of parents is to teach, to make their children conscious; children should make themselves conscious, they should try to learn. There is an implication here that nobody has complete consciousness, or, in its literal sense, that nobody has a complete soul, until he has become a fully participating member of the society. Even then, those who know more are considered to have stronger souls than those who know less, and through their knowledge and the strength of their souls, to have more potential for creating good or evil in the community. When a parent teaches his child how to till the land, how to cut timber, how to talk with his elders and his younger relatives, how to treat strangers, how to pray to the gods, in brief, how to deal with everything judged valuable by the community, it is said that the father is making his child become conscious of himself and of everything worthy of relating. The child should treasure this inheritance and later pass it along to his own children, for it makes life possible and keeps it safe from danger. Trouble makers are advised to recall their consciousness and act accordingly to the values of the society.

Learning, then, is intimately tied to the environment, to the community, and to the daily round of activities. Children learn as they participate in the religious, economic, and social life of the community, contributing their share to the family's welfare. They learn to farm by farming, to weave by weaving, to communicate with the supernaturals by communicating (Arias Sojob 1970).

The Indians do not differ radically in their approach to teaching from Dewey and his later followers. They believe in learning by doing and in making learning meaningful in the broader context of community life.

In one sense, childhood draws to a close when all the sustenance activities are mastered, for the adolescent is expected to participate fully in the family's activities. In another sense it ends only with parenthood; this is especially true for women, for whom motherhood is equated with adult status.

LADINO CHILDHOOD

Although they deny it, most ladinos bring their children up in much the same fashion as Indians. This is especially true for the poorer ladinos, themselves generally only one or two generations removed from tribal life. Wealthier ladinos have servants to help with child rearing; these are usually poor ladinos but may be Indians recently moved from their lands. All classes are exposed to Indian child-rearing practices with only some modifications.

The major differences regard attitudes toward work, schooling, and the role of the male. Indians believe that laziness is sinful and bring up their children to be hard workers; ladinos, at least those of the upper classes, feel that while mental work befits a person of their status, physical work does not. Many Indians, too, expect to work with their backs, whereas ladinos are expected to work with their brains, seated in a chair all day (Colby and van den Berghe 1961). Pay rates in San Cristobal reflect this bias, with day laborers earning less than 10 pesos daily and maids even less; ladino secretaries earn 15 to 20 pesos daily, and other white-collar salaries rise from there. The ubiquitous store clerks, many of them acculturating Indians, begin with about 200 pesos a month.

With maids and houseboys to do manual chores, wealthier ladino children soon consider themselves above any manual labor and above those who must perform it. Rather, it is felt that their time should be spent in schooling and in entertainment. The wealthier almost always aspire to send their children on to university-level education and entry into a profession; this is especially true for the boys, although girls may be educated to become teachers or secretaries and then marry or, at least, become engaged before beginning to work. Thus even the girls of a wealthy family are likely to receive at least nine years of formal schooling, and more often twelve. There are two schools in San Cristobal offering preparatory level education, corresponding to the same level approximately as the Associate of Arts programs in the junior colleges of the U.S.A.

Another major difference between Indian and ladino styles of child rearing lies in the role of machismo. Machismo, in its classical form (Wolf 1959), is all but unknown among Indian men, although adultery is not uncommon. Not so with the ladino men, who are brought up to all the ideals and practices of machismo from earliest childhood.

Other notable differences between Indian and upper-class–ladino child rearing lie in distinct attitudes toward medicine, an avowed disbelief in witchcraft by the ladinos, and eagerness to practice child-rearing methods advocated by the broader Mexican community. It is only among the upper-class families that one is likely to find a copy of Dr. Spock or a similar child-rearing manual; often it is a well-worn copy. Also, although the wealthier ladino merchants do include their older children among their employees, there is less expectation that children will be companions to their parents or that they will inevitably continue in the family business. Instead, many possibilities for different careers are opened to them, or at least to the boys. An adolescent may help out in the family store during vacations and after school hours, as may his mother, but when it comes time for him to select a means for earning his living as an adult there is relatively little pressure placed upon him to take over in his father's place. An exception to this is found among the artisans, who often train their children carefully and expect them to continue their craft.

In almost all other respects ladino children are brought up like Indians. They do work, helping out in the family's business. Although women give birth in a small hospital, attended by a trained midwife, if they can afford it, they too enjoy extra bedrest and a special diet during the postpartum period. Some upper-class women elect to give birth at home; they are attended by the same midwife, for few want to be seen by a male doctor. Babies are held almost all of the day, although not as much by the mother as by a substitute. They are breast-fed and later given solid food on demand. They are comforted almost immediately, although often with a commercial pacifier which contains a bit of honey in it rather than with a breast or bottle. When it is time for babies to talk they, too, are given the tortillas with the special holes in them. Baptism is their first major fiesta, but saints' days are also celebrated every year with a special cake and the singing of "Mananitas." Older children, like their Indian counterparts, are encouraged to be companions and caretakers of their younger siblings. Indeed, the parallels between Indian and ladino child-rearing practices appear to be much greater than the differences, which appear to lie more in the realm of values.

4 / The schools

From the security of their homes, where parents try to keep danger at bay and where almost all learning takes place through observation, imitation, and exploration, somewhat over half of the children currently leave to spend several hours a day at elementary schools run by the federal or state governments.

THE DEVELOPMENT OF INDIAN EDUCATION IN MEXICO

Formal schooling for the Indians of the Chiapas Highlands gained its first real impetus during the Cardenas regime of the late 1930s. Prior to that time a few Indians attended schools in some of the tribal centers. The children usually were forced to attend and were virtual servants to the teachers. They were severely punished for failure to learn their lessons well and for other infractions of the rules, such as the use of the mother tongue even before they had learned any Spanish. Often they were made to kneel on pebbles or fruit pits for lengthy periods of time in order that their lessons might penetrate; many teachers punctuated their instruction with a leather strap or a thorny switch. Since most of the students in the village schools were ladinos, the Indians received considerable abuse from their classmates as well as from the teachers.

Indian parents did all they could to save their children from the terrible fate of attending school. For example, in Chamula, in the 1930s, school-aged boys were dressed as girls, at least when they came to market, so that they might not be caught and forced into school (Castellanos 1970); girls were not made to attend. There and elsewhere children were hidden in the forests, sometimes for days on end, so that the census-takers might not count them. Sad, indeed, was the fate of the child who had to attend school.

The Mexican rural school of the 1920s ("La Casa del Pueblo") developed primarily as a center for community development; its teacher was expected to bring all the zeal and energies of a missionary to his work. Poorly trained, underpaid, and overburdened, the teachers' lives were often threatened when their community action programs conflicted with the interests of the local ruling factions. However, these rural schools, while they are often remembered with great admiration and nostalgia, had relatively little immediate effect on the country; in 1931, 81 percent of the communities with less that 4000 people were still without schools, and, with the continual competition of child labor, only 2 percent of the students continued beyond second grade (Ruíz 1963:40–41).

During the Cardenas regime more rural schools were opened throughout the country than at any previous time in Mexico's history. It was during this period that federally-supported Indian boarding schools in San Cristobal, Amatenango, and Zinacantan were founded; among their students are most of the present Indian teachers.[1] A scattering of federally- and state-supported day schools was also opened in the Highlands in Indian communities. These were ostensibly modeled after the pioneering rural schools for mestizos developed during the preceding decade, but, in fact, were seldom staffed by persons genuinely interested in helping Indians.

In 1948 the National Indian Institute (INI) was founded as an outgrowth of the first Inter-American Congress of 1940 and the political labors of its director, Alfonso Caso. The first of the Highland schools to be opened under INI auspices date from 1952; their inception spurred the founding of more federal and state schools. In 1964 the administration and supervision of federal and INI schools merged. Both state sponsorship and supervision of some schools continue; they tend to follow federal policies and practices.

EDUCATIONAL POLICIES

Official educational policy was spelled out in the Constitution of 1917, which granted to all Mexicans free, obligatory, fundamental education and which stipulated that schools be founded for the economic, social, and cultural growth of the communities as well as the nation, free of all religious teaching.

In 1958, the Secretary of Education, Torres-Bodet, proclaimed a major educational reform, still founded on the needs of a growing nation; his policies continued in effect as recently as 1971. Among the themes stressed were the primacy of national over individual goals; the need for curriculum to be based on children's experiences and society's needs; and, in light of the reality of wholesale school desertions, the necessity for fundamental education to form the curricular core of the first four grades.

At the time of the Torres-Bodet Proclamation of 1958, Highland education officials of all three systems, INI, federal, and state, saw the school as the focal point for community development. Of the three, however, it was the INI which stressed this aspect most, for its primary concern has always been the modernization and industrialization of Mexico. It sees the acculturation of the Indian as a means to that end and expresses an interest in the well-being of the people with whom it deals, especially through raising economic levels and enhancing the "positive" aspects of Indian culture (Romano 1964:31–34).[2] Within this framework and in addition to the philosophy advocated by the Secretary of Education, the INI advocates the

---

[1] The schools in Amatenango and Zinacantan later closed their boarding operations. A new boarding school for girls was later opened in Zinacantan.

[2] By "positive" aspects of culture, INI officials mean those aspects of Indian culture which coincide or, at least, do not clash with the Mexican national culture.

use of the mother tongue for beginning instruction (as a vehicle for more effective learning of Spanish) and relies upon the schools as the primary agencies of acculturation (Montes 1954). The Secretariat of Education adopted the INI program for initial instruction in the mother tongue in 1964, leading to a merger of INI and federal administration and supervision. Although all other ethnic differences are largely ignored, at this time all schools in Indian communities are expected to begin instruction in the vernacular (Plan de Educación Indígena para 1964). Reading primers are now being provided for fourteen of the fifty Indian languages spoken in Mexico, including Tzeltal and Tzotzil. In the Highlands many of the school inspectors encourage the use of the vernacular; wherever bilingual teaching personnel are found some initial instruction in reading is given in the vernacular along with oral instruction in Spanish.

Federal schools are centrally administered, with most direction coming from the offices of the Secretariat of Education in Mexico City. For each state there is a Federal Director of Education; under his supervision are the inspectors for each of the school districts or zones. Below the zone inspectors come the directors of the primary schools, generally teacher-directors. Under the supervision of these school directors are the group teachers, known as assistants.

Training is being conducted in Mexico on many fronts. Until 1971 the Secretariat maintained an institution for in-service training, the Institúto Federal de Capacitación del Magisterio, and a department for curriculum research and dissemination, Consejo Nacional Técnico de la Educacion (UNESCO 1953: 707).[3] The INI gave orientation courses to new bilingual teachers.

For the state system there is the State Director of Education and local inspectors; in 1972 there was one State Inspector for the entire Highlands. So far there has been no merging of the state and federal–INI systems although this seems in the offing. Since most state schools are located near roads it is easier for the State Inspector to visit his schools than it is for most of the federal or INI inspectors, who may travel by horse or foot for a whole day to reach the more distant schools; at the time of the field survey (see Chapter 5), when the Ocosingo highway had not yet been built, it took two days by horse or foot to reach some schools.

The primary task of the inspector is to improve the quality (and quantity) of education, stressing national goals over the needs of individual students or teachers. Those working out of the federal office (there were four in 1972) are expected to ". . . orient, direct, advance, and measure educational work . . . in the following areas: educational, sociological, administrative, material (building and equipping the school), and in-service training" (Garcia Ruíz 1963:147, 151). They are expected to visit their schools at least twice a year, seek solutions for school and community problems, and teach and illustrate those solutions (Garcia Ruíz 1963: 154–155). Both federal and INI-trained teachers are under their supervision.

Inspectors working out of the INI office (also four in 1972) are expected to do

---

[3] Major changes appear to be forthcoming in both policy and administration at this time (1973). The shape they will take and whether they bode good or ill has yet to be determined. In 1970, at the beginning of the Echeverría regime, the INI's educational office passed entirely into the Federal Secretariat of Public Education, to be maintained as a new and somewhat independent office.

much the same and to make monthly reports of the above activities to the (INI) Director of Education (Romano 1964:35).

It is expected that all schools be erected by locally donated labor and/or funds. Federal and state school buildings are either adobe and tile ranch-style buildings (Juarez type) or are prefabricated, mass-produced, and more modern in design and materials. The Secretariat advocates 1.35^2 or 5.4^3 meters of space per pupil, with at least one fifth of wall space on the pupils' left devoted to windows and with floors of some material other than dirt. A rural school building may also contain living quarters for the director and his family (Gallo M. and Guitíerrez 1963; Secretaría de Educación Pública 1963).

In addition to classroom buildings the Secretariat lists the following as highly desirable annexes, to be constructed as a community can afford them:

1. *Recreational:* Open air theatre, basketball and volleyball field, playground, and a yard for organized group games
2. *Vocational:* Farm field, vegetable garden, orchard (if only for a few fruit trees), flower garden, pens and cages for domestic animals, workshops (for activities such as carpentry, bookbinding, toymaking, smithy, tinwork, and, when raw material is found in abundance, basketry)
3. *Sanitary:* Latrine, bath, clinic
4. *Cultural:* Museum, library, science laboratories, reading room, public secretary
5. *Domestic Activities:* Sewing, cooking, laundry
6. *Other:* School office, administrative office, store room

It is also desirable to build a storehouse and a separate kitchen for each teacher and (when the breakfast program was in existence) a kitchen and dining room for students (Gallo M. and Guitíerrez 1963).

Schools built by the INI (the so-called INI type) are generally long, stucco buildings, oriented on a strict north–south axis to allow maximum sunlight through large prefabricated doors and windows, which are placed approximately one meter apart on both the long east and west walls. The buildings should be covered by two-sided tile roofs and floored with wood, brick, or cement, depending upon local materials (Acción Indigenista 1960, 1962). The schedule for annex constructions is much the same as for the federal schools, if on a more modest scale and with the addition in each school of special rooms for housing visitors. In the few boarding schools[4] there are dormitories.

The Secretariat of Education is expected to supply the following educational materials to its schools: free textbooks for all students; notebooks; chalk (white and colored) and erasers; pens and ink; a set of thirty-two maps; pictures of national heroes; poster paper; geometric models; tools for drawing geometric figures on blackboard; and paper.

---

[4] There have been several semiboarding schools in Indian communities, the number varying from one year to another. When open, they operate in combination with local day schools, but provide housing for third- to sixth-grade students who live too far away to walk to school every day. In addition there are two centralized boarding schools drawing their students from all corners of the Highlands although Oxchuqueros predominate in each. Boys attended the San Cristobal School, founded in the 1930s, while girls attended a new school in Zinacantan which was opened in 1968. In 1972 the Zinacantan school was made coeducational; the next year, the San Cristobal School admitted girls and moved to Ocosingo.

In addition, the federal government sets the standards for construction of desks and benches for students and for the construction of blackboards for teachers' use (Gonzales 1965). It is assumed that rural communities will construct their own furniture or pay for its construction (Gallo M. and Guitíerrez 1963).

Before the federal–INI merger, the INI supplied its schools with much the same materials as did the Secretariat of Education, except for the poster paper. In addition, however, INI also supplied letter and number masonite flash cards; flannel boards; small colored sticks (for the teaching of colors and numbers); and posters (dealing with matters of health and sanitation).

The State of Chiapas supplies no equipment to its schools; it apparently has not done so since teachers' salaries were raised in 1936. Whatever equipment and supplies are seen in the schools are supplied by the parents and teachers (F. Santiago 1965).

Fifty is the generally accepted class size throughout Mexico; nationally, enrollments average about forty-eight, although rural classes tend to be larger, and daily attendance averaged forty-one per group of fifty in 1967 (Secretaría de Indústria y Comercio 1968).

There is not much correspondence between age and grade placement. The age of initial school enrollment varies considerably, especially in the rural areas. Promotion is supposed to be based upon the passing of end-of-year examinations. Prior to 1960, about 30 percent of all primary students had repeated a grade once; students beyond fourteen years of age are not supposed to be enrolled in day schools, but, in 1959, 23 percent of the fourteen-year-olds were enrolled in the first grade (Flores 1961:32–39). In 1967, 31 percent of primary school children were enrolled in first grade nationally, but first-graders made up almost half of the enrollment in the rural schools of Chiapas. Almost 70 percent of first-graders were promoted both nationally and in the Chiapas rural schools. Nationally, 8 percent of primary-school enrollees were sixth-graders, but in the rural schools of Chiapas sixth-graders formed only 1.5 percent of the primary-school population (Secretaría de Indústria y Comerico 1968). In 1959, approximately 52 percent of primary students throughout the nation were boys and 48 percent were girls (Flores 1961:32).

There is little in the way of printed material on the nature of teaching personnel available for Mexico. It is known, however, that there is a shortage of teachers. In 1959 there were estimated to be over 3 million primary-school–aged children in the country (Flores 1961:29); it is estimated that there are now over 12 million primary-school–aged children. If there were one teacher for every fifty children between the ages of six and fourteen, there would be over 240,000 teachers at work. In 1965, approximately 152,000 teachers staffed the schools; by now, at approximately a 6 percent average annual increase in teaching personnel, there may be about 223,000 primary teachers.

In order to provide as much personnel as possible, educational requirements for entering the teaching profession were relaxed for a time to include graduates of secondary as well as of normal schools (Secretaría de Educación Pública 1963:111). In addition, bilingual primary-school graduates might be hired to teach beginning classes in the mother tongue. All teachers who had not completed normal school were strongly encouraged to do so through special classes on weekends (if they lived close enough to an in-service center) and school vacations, and were rewarded with salary increases and tenure. The in-service training was supplied by the Institúto Federal de Capacitación del Magisterio; in 1963, almost 29,000 teachers were enrolled in its classes, and the number rose considerably until that institution was dismantled.

The Eleven Year Plan (*Plan de Once Anos*) outlined by Torres-Bodet in 1959 envisioned a gradual increase in classrooms and in teaching personnel, with the hope that every group of fifty children would have a teacher and a classroom by 1970. It appears that much progress was made but that the goal has not been completely met.

The federal government is now reputed to pay its teachers between 1310 and 1860 pesos monthly[5] in both urban and rural schools (Secretaría de Educación Pública 1963:115), the differences being due to the remoteness of the area and other hardships associated with the zone in which the school is located. In 1967, teachers who held normal school certificates were reported to average 1424 pesos monthly; uncertified teachers were paid less (Secretaría de Indústria y Comercio 1968). In addition to teacher, the Secretariat lists the position of *promotor* for bilingual primary-school graduates, a position for which it pays a salary of approximately 800 pesos monthly. The INI pays about $600 to its *promotores*.

Mexico's stereotype of a primary-school teacher is that of a very overworked man. Most Highland teachers, Indians and mestizos alike, are men.

The INI hires promotores only, although many of the teachers who were originally hired for that position (110 in 1964) have since been placed on the federal payroll (as assistants or directors). Many of the promotores originally hired by the INI, when it first began to establish schools in the early 1950s, were barely literate themselves. Since 1965, there have been more applicants than positions for promotores, and the INI now requires both primary-school certification and a minimum age of 18 for the candidates. Teachers are expected to work at least 200 days a year, giving classes either from 9 A.M. to 5 P.M. with a three-hour break during the early afternoon, or in a single five-hour session beginning at 9 A.M. with a half-hour recess at noon. Classes are generally held Monday through Friday. There is a high rate of teacher absence so that few classes actually meet over 175 times in a given school year. In the Highlands all teachers of Indians are expected to attend training sessions two weekends a month and generally need at least the preceding and following days for travel to and from their schools.

When Torres-Bodet proclaimed the educational reform in 1959 he called for major changes in teaching methods and curriculum, with content to be related to children's daily lives and with teachers expected to use first-hand experiences and a "global" approach closely akin to our "activity" method (Villareal 1962:38), which

---

[5] The Mexican peso is worth $.08 U.S. currency, but has more buying power for food and shelter and other important needs. Despite this, the scale of living enjoyed by most teachers, especially those working in the major urban centers, is much lower than that common among North American teachers. On the other hand it is considerably higher than that of most Highland Indians.

requires participation in actual projects. The reformed curriculum advocated six areas of study:

1. Health education
2. Natural sciences
3. Social studies
4. Creative activities (art, music, and dance)
5. Practical activities (shop and domestic sciences)
6. Elements of culture (reading, writing, and arithmetic)

No mention was made of creative language or mathematical activities (Consejo Nacional Técnico de la Educación 1962).

The daily schedule should begin with general activities, such as health and room inspection, attendance, and perhaps patriotic ceremonies. These were to be followed, in turn, by a "systematic" study of the sixth area (the three Rs), to include both formal lessons and drill. The remainder of the school day should be divided among the remaining five areas, perferably in a global fashion (Villareal 1962:145).

Discipline problems were apparently ignored by the authors of the program. The assumption appears to be that students would be quiet and docile, that lack of interest would be expressed by slight restlessness and a lack of learning, and that interest would be expressed by enthusiastic but quiet participation. There was no suggestion that the authority of the teacher might be questioned or ignored, just as there was no mention of discipline problems.

Omitted from the official program, but very much a part of schooling in many of the Indian communities of the Highlands, was the Preparatory Grade, during which time the children were expected to gain a firm hold of Spanish, to learn to read and write in their mother tongue, and to gain some notions of arithmetic. For the preparatory year the promotores were encouraged by the INI to use a variety of instructional materials, such as flannel boards, flash cards, colored sticks, and lottery games, to better elicit the learning of the second language, arithmetic, and, most of all, literacy.

Reading, as such, should be approached "globally," through phrases and short sentences prior to the analysis of individual words and letters. The primers, however, follow a phonics approach. The first lesson contains only one consonant and a minimum number of vowels set in a paragraph-length story. Thereafter each of the other letters is introduced in a new lesson and drilled in a systematic fashion; previously taught letters are reviewed through short stories. Special primers in Tzeltal and Tzotzil were supplied by the Secretariat of Education until 1970 and again in 1973 for this purpose; they were to be augmented both by the use of some of the instructional materials listed above and by the writing of words and phrases. Using primers, students are taught to write in manuscript, forming the letters exactly as they see them. The children are not expected to understand the use of capitals or punctuation.

It is specified that Spanish be taught orally, largely through choral speaking, the vocabulary to consist of objects that are a part of the child's life such as those found in the classroom or the natural environment and the parts of the body. Teachers should use complete sentences and children should respond first with words and later with phrases. There is no specified vocabulary list (Montes 1954).

It is expected that a minimum of one hour daily be devoted to oral Spanish. Reading, writing, and arithmetic should also be taught daily.

The INI, like the Secretariat, expects the teachers to be authoritarian, albeit benign. It, too, expects acquiescent pupils, but it does make some note of discipline in its official program. Teachers should treat their pupils gently, use no corporal sanctions, and avoid punishment altogether whenever possible (Montes 1954).

After the preparatory year, the curriculum (entirely in Spanish save for explanations in the mother tongue during the first grade) is outlined in the federal textbooks, workbooks, and instructional manuals. The first grade should include an introduction to reading, primarily phonics-oriented. First the vowel sounds are learned, then the consonants, blends, and the irregular or foreign letters (such as x, w, and k), proceeding from the easiest to the most difficult. Each of the lessons also contains drill materials consisting of short stories that reinforce previous learning as well as the letter being studied. By the end of the first grade children are expected to know the entire alphabet and to be able to decode. They should be able to read the print of the texts and to write in cursive style, using both small and capital letters, as well as to use periods, question marks, and exclamation points. They should also know some simple grammatical rules, primarily those of gender.

In the second year silent reading is introduced, as is reading comprehension and the interpretation of written materials. Handwriting should be improved, students should be able to take simple dictation,[6] free composition is begun, previous work is reviewed, and more grammatical rules (number and gender) are included. There is a review of some of the irregular letters in the orthography (r, rr, g, and c), accents, and more punctuation marks (Instítuto Federal de Capacitación del Magisterio 1964; Domínguez and Leon 1962; Castro F. 1964). As indicated before, there is no mention in the federal materials, which are also used in the state schools, of preparatory classes for non-Spanish–speaking pupils. The third and fourth grades are more demanding academically, and the fifth and sixth even more so, generally paralleling curriculum in the United States. Relatively few children attend the Chiapas rural schools beyond second grade.

Pupil promotion is based on end-of-year examinations. Sixty-eight percent of children in federal and state schools throughout the nation in 1959, including new entrants to first grade, had never failed a year's work, nor had 66 percent of those who had dropped out before completing primary school. This means that approximately one-third of children in the primary schools had failed at least once. When new entrants into first grade are discounted, 47 percent failed at least once, and 18 percent failed four or more times. Of this 18 percent, almost half had never progressed beyond first grade (Flores 1961:37). It appears that the children are not failing as much now as they did prior to the Educational Reform (Secretaría de Indústria y Comercio 1968). Parents should be informed of their children's progress by means of monthly as well as final reports, with numerical grades for all six areas of the curriculum (six through ten are passing grades).

---

[6] Dictation is a popular curriculum activity throughout the nation. Prior to the distribution of free textbooks, beginning in 1961, teachers in the poorer communities had to rely upon dictation to provide their students with study materials. Since then it is still favored as excellent practice for spelling, punctuation, handwriting, and the acquisition of an elegant writing style.

Areas of autonomous behavior for the teachers are not spelled out, although it is expected that they will adapt their lessons to meet the needs of their students (Paz Sarza 1964). In general the strictures of the federal books are considered minimal, to be covered by all teachers, but to be augmented by additional experiences, drills, and assignments.

THE SCHOOLS IN OPERATION

In 1964 to 1965 a field survey was undertaken which included day-long to week-long visits to twenty-six schools (see Chapter 5 for the selection procedures). The following section is based primarily on that sample of twenty-six schools, as they were observed in the field study and in later visits through 1973.

The policies that had been outlined by Torres-Bodet appear to determine many of the educational practices observed. All of the twenty-six schools owned and used the free federal textbooks. All but one of the teachers interviewed claimed to follow federally or privately published manuals that advocate a highly nationalistic program that stresses the Mexicanization of the students. All of the teachers taught in Spanish, many of the bilinguals abandoning use of the local tongue for any instructional purposes whatsoever after the first grade.

In order to provide the universal education outlined in the National Constitution, school directors were ordered to take a yearly census and to enroll all school-aged children on the census lists. In practice this was rarely the case. Two state schools had official enrollments of fifty, since fifty students per teacher is the correct ratio and there was only one teacher per school; actually both enrollment and attendance were well above that figure! Other school censi listed only some of the children of the community. This was most apparent when the teacher was new to a community or otherwise lacked the confidence of his neighbors. Teachers report that some parents herd their children into the house, close the door, and deny that they have any children. Nowadays those parents who do send their children to school are much more prone to complain than they were in the past if they feel their children are being mistreated by the teachers, some parents going so far as to see the Federal Director of Education for the State of Chiapas. School is not as much feared as it once was.

In all but the state schools the census lists were taken to be the official enrollment lists, but other, more accurate, lists were also drawn up. School enrollment varies from one tribe to another and also reflects the popularity of each of the teachers. In some tribes, such as Chamula, relatively few children are enrolled in school. For a total population of over 45,000 (29,333 according to the 1970 census),[7] of whom perhaps 10,000 are of elementary-school age, there were only

---

[7] The population figures for Chamula were derived in the following manner: In 1960, the census listed about 26,000 for Chamula. Various anthropologists estimated the actual population at closer to 40,000, based on the numbers of children and others we knew to be absent from the census lists. This may actually be far too conservative a figure. The 1970 census listed 6743 school-aged children. Taking into account the 26:40 ratio of the 1960 census there are probably about 10,000 school-aged children in the tribe. The 26:40 ratio was not modified for this calculation because, while on the one hand, it is precisely the school-aged children who are most often hidden from the census takers (thus altering the ratio), it is also true that resistance to schooling has decreased somewhat and it is likely that a smaller percentage of children are being hidden now than formerly.

Sewing lesson in Oxchuc. The woman in western dress and the man standing next to her are the teachers.

sixty schools in 1970 with a total enrollment of 5018 for the whole tribe. About half of the children, especially the girls, were not enrolled in school. In contrast, however, about four-fifths of the school-aged children in Oxchuc, girls as well as boys, do attend (Cruz Santiago 1971), and almost all appear to attend for at least two or three years while of school age.

The academic program rarely extends beyond the fundamental education of the early grades; the other academic and cultural aspects of the program are generally ignored. Literacy is stressed and is considered to be the essential base for the economic and cultural development of the community. Group singing and dancing and basketball games are the most commonly organized nonliterary activities. There is also much stress on the highly abstract notion of nationalism; all schools hold weekly assemblies devoted to patriotic ceremonies, and much attention is paid to national heroes and commemorative days.

As applied, the curriculum appears to be only slightly related to the children's experiences. This is particularly noticeable in the Language Arts program, which uses Spanish in the teaching of all subjects beyond the preparatory year. By using Spanish the teachers tend to put comprehension of the subject matter beyond the children's reach; some teachers said that they had been instructed by their inspectors to drop all use of the local language by second grade in order to speed the mastery of Spanish.

Minimal curriculum modifications for rural education were observed, consisting primarily of the maintenance of school agricultural plots that were used to teach a minimum of farming techniques and to raise money for the school. Physical education was limited largely to marching, some calisthenics, basketball, and volleyball. Other sports are excluded because they either require equipment which is prohibitively costly for the communities or require large playing fields which are too difficult to dig with pick and shovel from the steep mountainsides. Soccer, the national game of Mexico, requires the use of shoes, which few, if any, of the children possess (Santiago M. 1965).

Contact between the teachers and their communities was maintained not only directly through the children, but also through local Education Committees, consisting of a president and two or more assistants. At least one committee member is expected to be present at the school during every school day. It was my impression that most committee members were loyal in fulfilling their duties; often three were present when I visited, although they were seldom warned in advance of my arrival. Among other responsibilities, the committees are supposed to help maintain adequate attendance, keep the school building and furnishings in repair, build additions as needed, bring supplies from San Cristobal (generally carrying them on tumplines for one or two days), and organize parent meetings and fiestas. When the work proves to be more than the committee itself can handle, such as in building additions to the schoolhouse, it is expected to organize work groups among the members of the community. To be chosen as a member of the committee is both an honor and a heavy burden.

Teachers are expected to supply leadership to the communities. Most Indian teachers appear to work well with their communities; most mestizo teachers appeared to have difficulties, either because of negative attitudes or because of the language and cultural barriers separating them. There were exceptions in both groups, however, for some mestizos worked quite well with their committees, while some Indians did not.

In addition to leading the committees in regard to their school-related functions, the teachers are expected to consult with the committees about community development projects such as piping in drinking water, establishing classes in baking or in the use of the sewing machine, and for adding on constructions to the school. Recently there has also been considerable emphasis placed on the organization of adult literacy classes in the afternoons.

Although it is expected that the inspector visit each of his schools at least twice a year, some teachers told me that they had not been visited at all for two years prior to my visit. Others said that they were visited as many as five times during the previous year. It was my impression that the inspectors varied considerably in their zeal and that the frequency of their visits was also governed by the accessibility of the schools. It was also my impression that most visits were either planned to deal with major attendance problems or were rather cursory in nature. There appeared to be little attention to improving the quality of instruction, although I was told that some inspectors did hold training seminars in San Cristobal. There was no way to judge the efficacy of these seminars, but nothing new which may have been advocated was observed in the field. Many teachers said they were eager for more help than they received, although few seemed to make much use of whatever help was offered. Many teachers also indicated a lack of confidence, even clashes, with their inspectors. At the same time, many inspectors complained of an overload of paper work which kept them from giving as much time as they wished to more direct supervisory activities.

During the field visits it was discovered that many school buildings, once too big for their few pupils, were now bursting at the seams. This was especially true of the INI schools, where two or three classes were crowded into space originally designed for one. Some federal and state schools were housed in wattle-and-daub huts with dirt floors, thatched roofs, and just a few tiny windows; these buildings were very dark inside and overcrowded. Situations were observed in which many new buildings were in use prior to their completion. Eight out of the twenty-six schools visited had dirt floors, and seven had gaping holes where windows were yet to be installed. Wherever attendance was high the classrooms were quite crowded.

All schools had a parade ground that usually also served as a basketball and volleyball court; a few had separate sports fields. Many federal schools did have some permanent facility for theatrical events, as did only one INI and one state school. A farm plot, vegetable garden, or orchard, or more than one of these, was found in about 75 percent of the schools, especially those founded by the INI. There were no animal pens in any of the schools, and only two flower gardens (both in state schools). Less than a third of the schools had carpentry shops, but even there the tools were often missing or broken. It appeared that when the men of the community undertook a carpentry job they then stocked up on tools or improvised them of local materials (many a time stones were used as hammers). It did not seem that either students or parents were encouraged to use the workshops. The same did not appear to be true for the four schools (one federal and three INI) where sewing machines were found. Times were set for instruction and the use of the machine, which was generally stored in a teacher's home. These sessions were well attended. Only two public laundries were encountered, these both in INI-founded schools.

Latrines were found in all but two of the schools (most latrines were in serviceable condition); four schools (one federal and three INI) had showers. No clinics were encountered, although they would have been welcomed; I was approached for medicine in many of the schools.

Attempts to encourage literacy and "culture" often went astray. Only nine of the schools had any books other than texts, and these were all adult books intended for highly literate persons. There was no evidence of their use by even the literate members of the community (even the most literate of whom, including the teachers, might have had considerable trouble reading them). One state teacher had made an attempt to establish a museum. Teachers were generally available to their communities as public secretaries; it was my impression that they rarely charged for their services, especially in communities located far from San Cristobal.

All school facilities included some form of housing and cooking facilities for their teachers, varying from several well-constructed buildings, including one six-room stucco building intended to house several families, to dilapidated shacks or a partitioned section of a classroom. All schools had some facilities for preparing the free school breakfasts being distributed in 1964, but only two had actual dining facilities. In the majority of schools the children ate on the patio. Almost all visitor's quarters had long since been usurped by the need for additional classroom and housing space, but four schools still combined a school office with visitors' quarters.

All schools supplied some form of seating and writing surfaces for the children, but the quality and quantity varied greatly from one place to another. As enrollments have risen furniture has become more scarce. The only classrooms in which children were not seen squeezed three or four to a desk designed for two were those where attendance was minimal at the time of my visit. The quality of the furniture varied from new and standardized to broken, unfinished, or inappropriate in size. Often tables and benches appeared to have been newly hacked into shape with machetes. All the furniture was wooden and appeared to be poorly constructed; in almost all of the schools some (in a few cases all) of the students sat on backless benches rather than on chairs.

All of the schools provided some form of blackboard for teachers, but, again, they were generally of poor quality; in some the board was merely a piece of once shiny black oilcloth tacked on a wall. Blackboards were generally hard to write on and harder to read, but gave evidence of much use. Slightly over half the schools had some additional furniture for the teacher, such as an adult-sized table and chair. Only two bookcases were encountered in all of the twenty-six schools visited.

All of the schools had the free textbooks, but often these did not correspond to the students' grade placements or to their skills. Pictures, charts, or maps were found in only about half of the schools, primarily those founded by the INI. Large demonstration devices, such as oversized clocks or counting frames, were found in only half of the schools (again, primarily those of the INI). Educational games, such as word or number lotto, a picture game similar in structure to bingo, were found in only six out of the twenty-six visited; local materials that could be adapted for teaching, such as the previously mentioned museum or collections of stones for number work, were found in only three. There was only one typewriter, this in a state school.

Classes in schools founded by the federal or state systems averaged fifty-eight in enrollment, of which 30 percent were girls; average attendance was thirty-nine, or 67 percent of enrollment; 28 percent of those attending were girls. In schools founded by the INI, average class enrollment was forty-three, of which 36 percent were girls; attendance averaged twenty-seven, of which ten were girls.

No reliable data was available on the children's ages. The students were almost always uncertain of their chronological ages, usually guessing, often quite wildly; other estimates, such as the teacher's or mine, were at least as inaccurate. Although the official school leaving age is fourteen, adolescents who looked considerably older were encountered in all the schools. It was my impression that any person who presented himself for enrollment as a full-time day student was accepted regardless of age. Young men, possibly eighteen or nineteen years old, were encountered as full-time students in almost every school.

Most of the teachers were men. Indian women applying for teaching jobs are snapped up, but they are a minority among the teachers; mestizo women formed an even smaller minority during the field survey. It was not possible to estimate the Indian: Mestizo ratio among the teachers, but the general pattern throughout the area has been to have both Indian teachers (to teach the lowest grades) and mestizos (at higher levels) work in schools with more than one teacher. Some inspectors, especially those working out of the INI office, favored Indian over mestizo teachers for all but the highest grades. One or two of the federal inspectors were known to avoid hiring Indians when at all possible.

Slightly over half of the INI teachers visited in 1964 and 1965 were on the federal payroll; by 1973 the percentage of federally paid teachers was much higher. All such teachers and all but two of the state teachers estimated their take-home pay as approximately 1000 pesos monthly; promotores estimated their take-home pay to be about 700 pesos. It is difficult to estimate the actual buying power of these salaries, but rural teachers were expected to maintain a standard of living almost as low as that of the rest of the community. Salary payments were often irregular, frequently delayed for months, sometimes a full year or more, during which time teachers were free to borrow at high interest rates. Since 1965, there have been some federal teachers, all normal school graduates, who have reported considerably higher salaries. In 1965 the two state teachers not being paid according to the federal scale received less than 200 pesos ($16 U.S. currency) monthly. Some of the more overworked state teachers also pressed their wives into assisting them without additional income. Regardless of the salaries they actually do receive, all teachers are considered rich by other Indians.

In 1964–1965, INI teachers ranged from new appointees to those who had been with the system for the twelve years it had been in existence, averaging five years of experience. Federal and state teachers ranged from new appointees to one who had been with the system for twenty-three years, averaging seven years of experience. Some INI teachers had had only two years of primary schooling prior to their first appointment; newer ones had completed primary school prior to appointment. There were also two mestizo normal school graduates who had just been appointed to INI-founded schools. In the state and federal schools preservice schooling averaged nine years, also ranging from two to twelve years.

Teachers who had not completed normal school were strongly encouraged to finish their professional training. Of the twenty-three INI teachers who were neither new appointees nor graduates of a normal school, there was an average attainment of one year's additional schooling in two. The average scholastic preparation of the INI teachers in 1964–1965 during the field study was nine years, ranging from six to twelve. Thus it appeared that all INI teachers, other than the new appointees or normal school graduates, had had some in-service schooling. In the federal and state schools, of the nine teachers who had neither completed normal school nor were new appointees, there was an average achievement of one year's growth in five; the average scholastic preparation at the time of the field study was tenth grade.

Some teachers appeared to have excellent rapport with their students, to instruct with clarity of purpose and method, and to interest themselves in the academic growth of individual students. This was true of both Indian and mestizo teachers; it was true of teachers in all three systems, INI, federal, and state. In the majority of classrooms, however, a confused atmosphere predominated. In most state and federal schools the language barrier or other gaps in communication between teacher and students often appeared to be responsible. The recent normal school graduates, who were the only teachers who had received any instruction in the newer educational methods, were also the teachers most ignorant of the local language and culture.

Few teachers made any attempt to go beyond the explicit lessons set forth in the federal textbooks. It was my impression that pupils expected to digest a book page-by-page and believed that memorizing was the same as learning. This contrasts sharply with the Indian concept of learning and mastering, of "becoming accustomed" through the performance of real adult tasks. One informant said that the children are so confused in school that they don't know what else to do besides memorize. Memorization was highly stressed by all teachers, as it was in the days preceding the educational reform of 1961. Indeed, the only evidences of the reform were found in the use of the federal textbooks and in a few faded teacher- or pupil-made charts; it appeared that most of the charts were made during in-service teacher training.

The children generally appeared docile and obedient, as though striving to understand and please their teachers. This fits the cultural expectation, which stresses obedience or avoidance, but never outright defiance. Several instances of mestizo teachers slapping children were seen. It appeared that most of these punishments were caused by teachers' impatience rather than by students' misbehavior. No

Reading lesson, Oxchuc.

Waiting for school to begin, Chamula.

punishments witnessed were as severe as those reputed to pre-INI days, when children were made to kneel on stones or peach pits; were hit on their palms with rods or rulers, or on their legs with stinging thorny switches; were made to do extra maintenance work in the school or teacher's house; were locked up in the school house (for failure to finish an assignment); or, in the case of the boarding schools, were ordered to remain on their beds for one or two days (Arias Sojob 1970; Castro 1959; Guiteras-Holmes 1961).

INI teachers appeared better able to communicate with their students. However, their classrooms appeared to be at least as confused as those of the mestizo teachers, probably because they generally had little understanding of their subject matter or teaching methods. They often approached their school tasks in a highly ritualistic manner, as though the routines would of themselves bring about the desired learning. Indian teachers appeared to be generally more patient and respectful of their students than mestizos, although a number resorted to frequent scoldings and reproofs. Students appeared to be generally more relaxed with Indian than with mestizo teachers; when they disliked a teacher they were not as obedient outside the classroom.

The rate of teacher absences appeared quite high, although it was not possible to determine the absence rate with any precision. State and federal teachers were reputed to be absent much more frequently than the Indians; I saw little to either substantiate or negate this.

School hours were flexible and, except where a teacher was occasionally inspired to keep his class in session beyond the suggested time, were generally less than the five daily class hours prescribed by the educational authorities. Two schedules were followed: In schools supervised by the federal inspectors classes were held from 9 A.M. until 2 P.M., with a short recess during the course of the day; in INI-supervised schools the children met from 9 A.M. to 12 P.M., had a two- or three-hour break, and reassembled for a two-hour session in the afternoon.

The relaxation of school hours is not out of keeping with the local culture. Students had no clocks; teachers often did not have clocks or watches either. It was my impression that it was the INI teachers who held the longer sessions, for perhaps a total of four hours daily, while the state and federal teachers probably averaged about three and a half hours. These shortened hours, frequent teacher absences, and even more frequent student absences indicate that instructional time

At play during recess, Oxchuc.

Recess in Oxchuc.

was considerably shorter for Highland Indian students than is advocated by the Secretariat of Education.

With the exception of one federal teacher, some variant of the new curriculum was followed. Teachers usually guided themselves with a very detailed schedule of activities spelled out in the federal materials; however, even the most detailed of the instructional manuals does expect that the teacher add further drills. Teachers tended to concentrate on the first and last areas of the program (general activities and elements of culture—reading, writing, and arithmetic), with little attention to the remainder. Natural sciences and social studies, when handled at all, were dealt with in isolation, dryly, with assignments in the texts, teacher lectures, and written questions and answers, almost always in all but incomprehensible (to the students) Spanish. Social studies were stressed more than the natural sciences because of the heavy nationalistic emphasis of the schools. Most social studies lessons consisted of polemics about national heroes, who were never humanized, and the memorization and recitation of verses about the glories of the Mexican flag, which were all but meaningless to the students.

This rote, almost irrational approach was typical of most teachers for most subject matter, the major exceptions being reading and writing, where students had to demonstrate their skills before passing from the preparatory to the first grade. Occasionally INI teachers used the vernacular in social studies and natural sciences, although this was rare. It must be remembered that most of the INI teachers themselves understood little of the material, at least as it appeared in the textbooks, and that they generally had a poor command of Spanish.

During the preparatory year most teachers tended to follow the procedures outlined in the INI manual (Montes 1954), which calls for the use of a variety of materials. However, perhaps as many as one-third of the promotores gave only oral Spanish pattern drills and taught reading largely through memorization. Spanish lessons were usually held for at least an hour each day, and reading, writing, and number drills were included in most daily schedules.

Although a global approach was advocated (at least by the INI) in the teaching of reading, in practice, reading instruction appeared to be almost exclusively phonics-oriented, with some concern for fluidity in oral reading. The first Tzotzil primer begins with the vowel sounds; the first formal lesson is *mi mu?* ("Is it tasty?"). This is placed below a large black and white line-drawing of a man holding up a fruit and a boy looking at him. Isolated words, especially mi and mu, follow. After the introduction of the vowels in the Tzeltal primer, the first consonant lesson consists of *ji, ja* (fly; corn), each accompanied by its black and white line-drawing,

Recess at the edge of the Pan-American Highway, Zinacantan.

followed by isolated syllables. There are two books for each language, which cover all the sounds in common with Spanish and a few additional sounds too frequent in the language to omit if sentence length materials are to be used. After the children have shown that they can sound out all of the stories and have passed the primarily oral end-of-year exam, they are sent on to first grade and the federal textbooks.

The federal materials are generally unrelated to the lives of the children. For example, the first reading lesson after the introduction of the vowels is about a teddy bear; few Highland Indians have any notions at all about furry toy bears or, for that matter, about live bears. The text consists of *ese oso se asea asi* ("That bear cleans himself like this."), placed below a colored picture of a seated teddy bear; isolated words follow the sentence. While the lesson may be effective for teaching the letter S to mestizos, it is almost devoid of meaning for the Indian children.

Concern with reading comprehension does not appear to enter into such a program until second grade, when the children are told to copy written questions for which the answers can be copied directly from the text. Although the content of the more advanced stories is not as arrid as the teddy bear lesson, only rarely are experiences common to the Indians dealt with in these stories. Rather, it is assumed that while learning to read they will also learn about the world beyond their own communities. Jaime, a young Oxchuquero teacher, very well integrated into his community, was observed giving the following lesson:

He asked his class of about ten children, aged eight to thirteen, to open their readers to the story, "The Mailman." The book was printed on coarse paper; the story began with a large colored picture of a street scene (including a mailman) in a mestizo village. Jaime walked around the room, checking to see that all books were open to page 34. His voice was soft and patient even when he spoke quickly; the Tzeltal melody pervaded his Spanish.

As soon as he finished checking the books, he said in Spanish. "We're going to read a little while." He repeated this two more times. "For those who can't, we'll read it one by one later on." He then said something in Tzeltal and the children began reading, *soto voce* as he sat at his table facing the children, head in hand, and began to read to himself, his lips moving.

Since the first grade teacher who worked on the other side of the sheet which separated their two groups had not yet returned from San Cristobal with his wife and three little babies, his class was becoming quite noisy. Jaime went to the other side of the muslin curtain to chide the children and to give them some work. (Throughout the morning nobody seemed to pay any attention to the children in the preparatory grade, which was housed in a separate shack and taught by the wife of the first grade teacher. In truth, the couple were having a hard time returning. Only two weeks had passed since the birth of their third baby and the mother was finding it very difficult hiking over the steep trails, the infant slung on her back or nursing from her breast).

After Jaime had allowed enough time for his class to read their story, slowly but steadily, decoding as they went, he called them to attention again. "Have you finished? Good. We're going to come up here, one by one. . . . Let's see. You," and he pointed to the first boy, "let's go." He was a handsome child, about nine or ten years old, sporting a brand new, untorn shirt.

The boy looked around at the others and then, very seriously, he went to stand next to his teacher with his book open. Jaime told him to read "strongly," and moved the boy's book to a "correct" position. But with the first few words the child raised the book to hide his face. He read word by word, singsonging to stress the accented syllables. His pronunciation was relatively clear, but he seemed to pay little attention to meaning; the prepositions were read as loudly as the nouns. I sat perhaps 6 feet away, but could hardly hear him for the noise coming from the rest of the class. Jaime appeared to be completely absorbed in the story and in the boy's pronunciation. At one point the boy stressed the wrong syllable, and Jaime said it correctly; the boy copied him and continued reading the sentence. By now he had probably lost whatever thread of meaning there had been. The children in the front rows followed in their books for a while and then began to look around the room. Those behind me were busy trying to figure out my notes (which were almost entirely in English). This absorbed them quite a bit, but they also seemed well aware of everything else that was going on in the class.

When the boy finished most of the first page Jaime called on the one sitting behind him. The first boy smiled as he turned toward the group; his front teeth were missing, although he looked older than eight.

The next boy read much more softly; he was barely audible, even to Jaime, who kept urging him in Spanish, "Louder." But he continued on his dogged path, in much the same style as the first child. Meanwhile the first boy sat in his chair, hugging his knees, then put his feet back down on the floor while he first drummed along the side of his desk, then began leafing through the pages of his reader, looking at the pictures.

As the morning dragged on and one after another of the children read, barely audibly, the first boy read other sections of his book to himself, examined his hands, picked his nose, wrote with a miniscule pencil stub, watched the other children in the class, talked with those closest to him, made cat's cradles, stood on his chair to look out of the high window in front of the room, pulled a string through his mouth, pulled at his teeth with it, pulled it alternately through his mouth and his toes (no children were ever seen to wear shoes), yawned a few times, examined his book again, read in it, sucked his thumb, examined the ceiling, gave some papers to the boys behind him, asked permission of the teacher to leave the room (granted), and soon ran back in.

Jaime continued listening to individual children for well over an hour. Through most of it he attended to the child reading to him, only rarely staring at the most active and noisy of his group. Merely a look appeared to be enough to restore quiet. Then, as the last two children read, he began writing in his notebook.

Now he addressed the whole group, "Read it again. Pay attention. What does it say? 'Mailman.' Mateo, do you know what a mailman is? There are mailmen in the city. Not here. So, what does it say? What did the mother do? She says . . . she is a woman. She was very sad because she never received any letters from her husband. It says here, 'She never received the letter she expected.' She was desperate for her letter and very sad. What did she do when there was a knock on the door? She often interrupted her work to listen for that knock. Now she had a son, who was named . . . ? What was his name? [No answer] You read this, didn't you? What's the boy's name? [No answer] His name is Pedrito. Now, this Pedrito, what did he do when his mother was so desperate? [Jaime was very involved in his story, and had almost lapsed into a highly accented, even pidgin Spanish.] Well, Pedrito wrote a letter to his mother, that is, he wrote a letter. To his mama. That's what Pedrito did. [This repetitiveness is an essential part of Indian rhetoric.] What do you think of that? To comfort her, yes, to comfort her. And he said, 'Mama, don't suffer any longer.' Who said that? Who said those words to his mother, that she shouldn't suffer any longer? Pedrito. Yes. Pedrito." Jaime had become quite dramatic. On the word "suffer" his voice seemed to express all the suffering in the world; for "comfort" it was filled with love and kindness. And so he continued, his voice soaring to ever greater dramatic heights as he told again of how Pedrito tried to comfort his mother.

It was all in Spanish. When he finished he asked twice in Spanish and then once in Tzeltal if the children had understood. To the last question he finally got an answer, "Yes," in Spanish.

Next, he announced reading comprehension time, telling the children to reread the story; most of them obeyed while he walked out of the room, to find the materials for a makeshift chalkboard eraser.

Almost ten minutes later he returned with a folded piece of paper instead of an eraser. He asked the children if they were ready; they called out, "Yes." He erased the board, which was covered with work that had not been removed for three weeks since the school had closed for a teachers' meeting in San Cristobal and for the Easter vacation. Most of the children watched as he wrote on the board, copying from his notebook:
"Read carefully and answer.
1. Why was Pedrito's mother sad? _______________________________________
2. What did she do when there was a knock on the door? _______________
3. What did Pedrito do to console her? _________________________________
4. What did his letter say? ____
5. What materials do you need to write a letter? ____________________"
He told the group to close their readers and begin answering, then left the room. Some of the children wrote, others chatted quietly, fiddled, or helped one another. None attempted to write any answers.

Jaime returned, asking the group if they had finished. He walked around the room checking on their work, told them to write the answers as well, and left the room. Only a few attempted to write even one-word answers; all chatted with one another.

Jaime returned. "Those who have finished may bring their work up." He waited.

Only one boy was able to answer; he brought up his work while the rest waited quietly. Jaime called on another boy, the first one who had read, and quickly graded the work. The two boys compared grades as they returned to their seats slowly. Jaime tried to call the others up, but no one responded. He looked at a girl; she buried her head in her book, pretending to write. He then went to the first grade to quiet the children; the second graders jumped up trying to get the correct answers from the two boys. When he returned he asked, "Have you finished, Tomas? [No answer] Here it says, 'Why was Pedrito's mother sad?' In the lesson it says . . ." and he began to read the pertinent sections of the story, answering each of the questions and writing the answers in turn on the blackboard. He got no help from the children; only one had really understood. As the lesson ended, Jaime was smiling very sadly.

At this point a boy arrived from another hamlet with a written message for me. Jaime handed me the note, but he made no use of this opportunity to explain what a mailman is; few if any of the children appeared to have any concept of a letter carrier or his job.

The morning was drawing to a close. Jaime told the children, in Tzeltal, that they should find their classmates and make sure that there would be better attendance the next day. Now the children perked up. He took the attendance silently, and chatted informally with some of the children, all in Tzeltal. They were very responsive, answered freely and joked, often quite cleverly. When dismissed they sailed out of the door, whooping softly but gleefully as they left, trailing laughter behind.

A ladina teacher, again one who was very well liked by her community, was observed in another reading lesson.

The schoolhouse was a large stucco building, lighted by two small windows high on one wall and by open doors on the opposite wall. It is always dark and damp inside; when the mists come down (which they do almost every day in the rainy season) the room becomes very, very cold. Two teachers worked in the room, stationed, at opposite ends, often trying to outshout each other. Inés taught a combined first and second grade; there were only fifteen boys and no girls in her group on the day I observed. Almost all were shivering with cold.

"Are we ready? Open to page 33. Let's see. Let's see, Ricardo! Speak up, read loudly."

Ricardo, a ladino youth began to read laborously, "My father is a sailor. His face is dark. He walks a little peculiarly. He sits on a staircase and takes some things out of his suitcase. The bull is for Luís, the earrings for Mama; Anita wants these." Inés corrected his pronunciation of the last word several times, then called on the next boy, who read even more slowly. She corrected many of his words, which he tried to repeat after her.

At this point an Indian youth of about fourteen or fifteen entered the classroom and took his seat. Lorenzo was tall and slim, his clothing shabby and dusty. He smiled to his neighbor in back, trying to see which page they were reading. He was the next student to be called on, and stood smilingly. Inés reminded him to read loudly and quickly, and came toward him, tapping another child on the head as she passed, "O. K.! Now Juan." Lorenzo turned to watch, his little finger in his mouth, his foot tapping. Juan read, repeating the many words that the teacher corrected. Lorenzo sat down again, his book closed, pressing it to his nose, his mouth, then putting it into his desk. Inés asked one more boy to read. When he finished she told the class, "Sit down. Now we're going to take out our workbooks. Everybody, take out your workbook." Lorenzo took out his workbook and stood to see which page the other children were turning to, while Inés turned pages in both her reader and workbook. "Page 33." He sat again, his attention on the teacher's book while he scratched the back of his head. "On page 33, notice that all the words have *R*s. As in *María, marino*, also *cara, moreno, raro*. . ." She continued reading all the words in the selection with the letter *R* in them. "In the same way we're going to find on page 33 all the words, all the letters, all the words with the same letter. And we'll put them into order, into order, in the form of a little staircase [the children do know what a staircase is since there are some steps leading up to the porch of the schoolhouse], numbered from one to as many as there are. We'll write one, and then a hyphen. . . . Güerro [Blondy], Güerro, bring me some chalk [this to the young, quite dark, Indian committee-member sitting in the room]. One, a line, and the first word we find. And after we've found all the words, we'll underline, with a red pencil, the letter *R*. O.K., take out your notebooks. Are we ready?" She started to write on the board as she repeated her explanation. Lorenzo sat, eyes on the board, little finger in his mouth, straining to see. As she told the group to take out their pencils he felt in his pocket.

"Are we ready? Good. Let's write. . . . O.K. Ricardo, what are you doing, what are you waiting for? You don't have a pencil? What do you come to school for, Ricardo? Take out your notebook. All right, now are you ready? Lorenzo?"

"Yes," the boy mumbled, grabbing his pen out of his pocket, putting it back, then grabbing his pencil out of the other pocket. He began to write. The teacher kept up a running monologue of instructions. "The second word is marino. This isn't the first time you're writing; why can't you do it? Go on, go on," and again she repeated the instructions. "Let's see, Ricardo, what letter is this? *R*. And this? Also *R*, so let's find all the words. Now have you understood, or not yet?" And again she repeated the instructions, bending over Ricardo's book as she did. Throughout this Lorenzo constantly shifted his attention from his work to her and back again to his work.

"Let's see, Ricardo, how many words have you found?"

"Four." She asked him to name them, and then to repeat the list. "Do you want to repeat it, or not, but louder, because Juan still doesn't hear, nor is he doing what he is supposed to be doing." Ricardo read his list, then she had Juan read the three words he had found. Lorenzo continually shifted his eyes from the board to his work. She turned to him, "Let's see, you go to the board. You're going to write one of the words you found in your notebook. Go on. You're going to write." He moved to the board slowly, taking the chalk even more slowly. "Any of the four that you found, any of them." He wrote the number four on the board. "With what number should you start, with number four or with number one? So fix it; erase it. Write just the words you found in the workbook. Whichever of those you wish. Which word? Sit down. Let's see, Juan. Now don't be ashamed." Lorenzo sat smiling, hugging his hands between his knees, watching the board. Juan had further troubles at the board, always accompanied by the teacher's running commentary. Suddenly she turned to Lorenzo to ask him if Juan's work was correct. He stretched, mumbling, "No."

"Who would like to fix it?" Ricardo stood up, then Lorenzo, who moved forward to let him pass. Lorenzo was called to the board and wrote what the teacher dictated. At last the four words were listed, and the class was told to take out red pencils. Again not all the children were prepared. "Don't you like to bring your colors? Well, since you didn't bring them we'll put away the notebooks and instead copy what you just read, with clear letters, down to where we finished." She reviewed how they should head their work with the name of their hamlet and their own names, and she reminded them to copy the work just as it was with attention to capitals and punctuation marks. Of course, they would write in cursive style, not copying the print of the books. "You won't forget? You're to write silently and quickly." Lorenzo grabbed a pen in his pocket, took out another one, then opened his book, but it was the wrong one. As he began closing it, the teacher called, "What happened to you, what happened? You should all be writing this, quickly. Let's go. I said, let's go. Put away your notebooks, put them away," and she tapped Lorenzo on the head. He shifted his notebook over further, partially covering Ricardo's, and began writing. "You shouldn't write here. Here. Hurry up. O.K.? With clear letters. This letter looks like this one."

Meanwhile the class at the other end of the room had become noisier and noisier, until it was hard to hear Inés over the din. The ladino teacher who worked there with the preparatory grade used both Tzotzil and Spanish, but not a word of Tzotzil was used to clear up the confusion in Inés' class.

The mathematics program in the preparatory year consists primarily of learning the names of the numbers, at least through 10, in Spanish. Addition and subtraction combinations through 10 are also introduced. From the first grade on the mathematics program is somewhat similar to that proposed in North American textbooks, although there is little set theory.

Another Oxchuquero was observed teaching a "model" arithmetic lesson. There were only twelve children present that day in his first-grade class—six boys seated at one side of the room and six girls at the other, with much bare space in between. The children appeared to range in age from six to twelve years. Tomás, the teacher, asked the two men standing at the window, members of the parents' committee, to come in and join them.

"So, children, let's work. We're going to take up the matter of arithmetic, which is to say, numbers, and the concepts of much–little–nothing and high–low–tiny. Pay careful attention. We have, let's see, boys [calling to the boys, but pointing to the girls], 1,2,3,4,5,6. How many girls are there?"

A boy called out, "Three." Tomás said, "Six. Now let's count the boys—1, 2, 3, 4, 5 [he did not seem to notice his error]. How many boys are there? [Some called out, "Five."] Now, of which are there more, boys or girls? Isn't it true that there are more girls? The girls are winning. By one. Just by one.

"Now let's say this. We also have here, in this classroom, how many tables? How many tables are there in this classroom? Let's count them all, clearly, boys and girls, please." He repeated all of this in Tzeltal, and then led the counting in Tzeltal. Then he continued in Spanish, "We also said the number in Spanish, we said it. How many tables are there?" He then repeated the question in Tzeltal, and got answers in both languages. He began to have trouble keeping track of the number of tables in the room, including those not occupied by the children. At the same time he invited the committee members, in Spanish, to come into the room.

Then he had the children count, in Tzeltal, up to 10. The lesson continued. "Now let's see. Here we have this part [pointing to half of the room]. This is one part; this is the other part. [He moved about the room a great deal, signaling, touching.] These are the girls' tables and these are the tables of. . ?"

A boy who had been leaning all over his table until now sat up and called out, "Boy."

"Boys. Good we have here, we'll count again on this side, we're here on this side, to the left of the boys, this is the side of the. . ?"

"Girls," called out several of the children.

"We have 1,2,3,4. And here, how many tables are there? ["Four," called out several children.] Four tables. And here we have 1,2,3,4,5. Where are there more tables? Here, where the girls are. There are 5 here, and here 4. Here there are many, many. Many means *bayan*. Few, *ternas*. And here in the center how many are there? [A child called out, "None."] None. Here we have none. *Mayuk*. Here we have a few tables and here many. Where are. . ? Is it true that there are many boys or few boys? Few or many? Look carefully, there are 4 boys. How many did we say? 1,2,3,4,5,6; 1,2,3,4,5,6. Now they're counted. There are six boys and six girls. Where are there more? They're equal. Nobody wins, they are equal. But as for the table, yes, here there are few, and here many. Correct.

"Look carefully. Here we have. . . . We'll make some drawings, quickly." He drew some large squares on the board as he talked. The board was in remarkably good condition; it was easy to see the drawings. "We have on this land, look carefully, we have two parts. This is the land of Martin, and this is the land of Pedrito, and this of Manuel. Here we'll put, look, what letter is this? What letter is this? [A child called out "*A*"] No, how can that be? *M*, we call it. So this is Martin's land, this is Pedrito's land [writing a *P* in the block], and this is Manuel's. And this is a . . . tree. Look carefully. Good, here we have, whose land? Martin's. And whose is this? Pedrito's. And this? Good. Look carefully at Martin's land. There are many . . . trees. Many trees. And here few trees, and here none. What do we say here? Many trees. And here? Few trees. [The children called out the answers, echoing him, relishing the words.] And here there are? None.

"How many blackboards are there in the room? One. And how many teachers are speaking right now? One. Pay attention, pay attention.

"Let's see. If I were to happen to lose this. . . . What is it called? It's an eraser. Eraser. How many erasers am I holding up? One. Look carefully. Now how many am I holding up? None.

"How many people are there in the room? Many. Many people. [The children continued chorusing out the one-word answers.] And what's this called? Window. How many windows are there in the school? Many. Many." Several of the children used the wrong Spanish gender in responding, and he corrected them. They repeated the word still incorrectly. He continued discussing gender, explaining that all words that are preceded by *la* (the) should end in *a*; then he began to list further examples of feminine words. "Let's say, 'the table.' And this is a . . . bench. This is a bench. And these? Chairs. Now think carefully. How many chairs are there in this classroom? 1,2,3,4,5. How many benches? 1, 2, 3, 4, 5,6,7. [The children counted along with him.] Of which are there more, chairs or benches? . . . The benches. There are many benches in this classroom, and few . . . chairs. Chairs. Watch carefully: We have this concept that we have here many, few, and nothing. Pay attention. Let's see this, . . . Please, don't talk, there, you, Elena." He then proceeded to draw some oranges on the blackboard while he repeated what he had said in Tzeltal. The lesson continued in much the same vein, as he talked about the many–few–no oranges they might get at the upcoming fiesta in Oxchuc. Then he returned to Martin, Pedrito, and Manuel, calling them brothers who were tall, short, and tiny. After a presentation in Spanish he would repeat, although more succinctly, in Tzeltal. He then discussed more–fewer–no pears; the number of children in the first through fourth grades (there were two fourth-graders out of four present that day); many stars, but only one sun and one moon. This led to the following:

"We have also the clouds. Think carefully. Many clouds. Those over there are wispy. Over there they're black, others white, the ones below are rising. Why are they rising? Because the rain is evaporating. O.K., let's go back. We have here a moon, right?" and he drew one on the board. He then elicited the words for moon and stars in Tzeltal, drew several stars on the board, then reviewed the concept of many–few–none again, returning to count children in the room and the furniture. From time to time he would interrupt himself to again invite the committee members into the room, but they continued watching from the window.

At one point he called on individual children to give the answers, but they stood bashfully, barely whispering the correct words. He called on two boys to come up to the front of the room with him, and continued, "My name is Tomás; this is Manuel, and he is Roberto. Now, who is the tallest? ["Tomás," chorused out the children.] Who is the smaller? ["Manuel"] And who is the tiniest?" "Roberto," they called out, giggling at the discomfort of the two boys who had been singled out to stand before them. Tomás repeated the essence of what had happened in Tzeltal and continued. "Good. Thank you. Sit down. Now let's see whose turn it is. Here we have . . . what's his name? [Some of the children sang out, "*Petul*."] *Petul*, or you could say Pedro. And . . . Manuel. Let's see, who else hasn't had a turn? You, stand up. [The boy sprang up, a big smile on his face.]

The lesson continued with more review of relations and with the children recounting the tables, chairs, benches, boys, girls, trees, and so on. Then they counted the numbers up to ten in both languages. Tomás then had them raise their arms, first the left, then the right, then count their fingers. Again, he repeated in Tzeltal, at the same time writing the numerals 1 to 10 carefully on the board; he continued the lesson. "So we now have, let's see, all together: 1,2,3,4,5,6,7,8,9,10. [The children also said 11, but he ignored them.] Good. That's big enough. Well, I'll write a number here. Let's see who can say it first. What number is this? ["Five"] The girls won. What number is this? ["Ten"]

Again the girls. What number is this? ["Nine"] The same. And this ["Six"]
Let's see. Correct. Again the girls." And as he continued writing the numbers,
the girls kept calling out first, mostly because one of the boys repeatedly shouted
a wrong number. Tomás then pointed out to the children that he had written his
numbers in a straight line, in order, and suggested that they do the same.
"Attention, Paco. Doubled over in the classroom!" [This child had been
particularly restless.]

Suddenly the class was diverted by the noise of another group at recess, but
Tomás paid it no attention. He continued to write numbers on the board, and
then had the children put their heads down on their tables. Most of the boys were
quick to respond, while Tomás repeatedly told the girls to sleep, to lie down, and
go to sleep. As soon as all the twelve heads were down he reawoke the class. The
children laughed. "Let's get back to work. What number is missing here,
among all others? ["Four," called out a child.] That's a lie because here's the
four," giggling. "What number's missing? Quickly! ["None"] None, not one
number's missing. They're all here. Right? Isn't it true that we've been working?
So let's go on." He continued to draw the numbers on the board, including zero,
which he placed after the nine, at the same time eliciting from the group that
it was worth nothing. Then he drew three cats on the board.

"This is a . . . cat. What's it called in Tzeltal? ["*Mis*"] What kind of a cry
does a mis have? [A child meowed, and the group laughed.] Well, here there
are three cats. Look carefully, three. And this one is . . . crossed out! Look
carefully. There's a cross on this one. We put an X on it and it just dies. So
how many are left? Two. What happened to the other one? ["It died."] It
died of hunger. It died because it didn't find any rats. That's what happens, right?
Now we have this; watch carefully," and he drew some fruit on the board.
"We're going to call this, what are we going to call it? ["Kitty"] Look carefully."
And he repeated in Tzeltal. "We'll call it 'limes.' How many limes are there here?
Four. Which means that this lime died, and we ate it, right? And we ate this one,
too. How many remained? Two, right. Now, here we have some . . . we'll call
these marbles. How many are there? You can see them; they're very tiny, right?
Good. These are crossed out; we sold them. How many are left? ["Six"] Five
marbles. We sold three, or we lost them, so we have five left, just five with
which to play. So let's go on." Then Tomás reviewed the subtraction, in both
languages, went back to counting the children in the room, and erased some of
what he had drawn on the board. "Let's see if you remember this. This is a sign.
It's called. . . . It's called. . . . It's called . . . a plus sign; and it means to add.
And this sign . . . is minus, meaning to subtract. Roberto. [The boy walked to
the front of the room, his fly wide open, but none of the children appeared to
notice.] It looks like you're getting tired. We'll do some addition. Take out
your notebooks. First you'll do some subtraction. A clean sheet! A clean sheet!
That's what I want to see." He repeated his instructions in Tzeltal and put five
addition problems on the board, explaining in Spanish all the while, stressing
the plus sign which he made quite large. There were five addition problems in
all, none summing to more than ten.

"Let's see, everybody works. Let's begin to copy. Everyone with his own
work. Everyone with his pencil. This is so you can rest. Pure talk is tiring, boring.
So we have to do this, to change activities." The children wrote, most of them
with great concentration, their heads buried in their work. "Have you finished?"
One of the boys called out, "Yes!" "Good, collect the notebooks. Go ahead." As
he continued writing, the boy kneeled on his bench, turning to collect the notebooks of those sitting behind; then he moved to collect the others, finally saunter-
ing to Tomás' table. "Let's see. María, didn't you remember your notebook?"
He repeated in Tzeltal, called for the remaining notebooks, and began collecting.
Pedro Díaz Gómez has eight. Francisco Gómez Sánchez has eight. Juan Sánchez

has ten. And this notebook has no name. O.K., now the girls. This one has no name. Elena Sánchez Gómez has two; she has two, two. Don't you have a notebook? Alicia has eight. This one, two. O.K., raise your hand if you got six." (No children responded.) He then asked each one what they got. Three boys and two girls had passed, one boy and one girl had not handed in any work. Thus only five out of the twelve had done passing work. He did the examples at the board, explaining all the while in Spanish, then gave them five subtraction problems, without further explanation. Many children mouthed the numbers as they wrote, but few counted on their fingers. Tomás corrected the notebooks as the children finished, and had the same boy collect those he had missed. Again he read out the grades; three boys and all six girls passed, two boys failed, and one did not hand in his work. Tomás reviewed the work, pointing out that they hadn't understood everything. As soon as he finished he left the room; the children sat quietly, waiting, chatting with one another, leafing through their books, touching one another, and moving around in their seats. The lesson had lasted an hour and a half and now, at five o'clock in the afternoon, it was time to go home.

Social and natural sciences were largely ignored by the teachers of the earlier grades, who had trouble covering all of the textual materials in language arts and mathematics; rather they appeared to rely primarily on the school assemblies for the former and on the children's occasional work on the school's farm plot for the latter. Although many classrooms did have some posters related to these areas on display, they seemed to be largely ignored by the teachers.

Creative and practical activities, other than caring for the school's agricultural facilities, were encountered only rarely in any of the schools, be they federal, state, or INI. This was due, at least in part, to the lack of facilities and equipment. Group singing was the most common creative activity; it was generally led by a teacher who himself sang poorly, and was unaccompanied by any musical instrument. I was surprised by the quite melodious quality of the singing.

During the course of the fieldwork I heard a number of stories about teachers who administered and graded end-of-year examinations inaccurately so as to show higher academic achievement. During the fieldwork I regraded the reading comprehension sections of some end-of-year tests, occasionally allowing some teachers to help administer the familiarizing buffer tests of the battery (see Chap. 5). There were many indications that at least some of the teachers helped the children with their answers or scored inaccurately. However, the practice was probably frequent throughout the nation at that time and not reserved to the Highlands. More recently Highland teachers were sometimes required to exchange schools for testing, so that they no longer examined their own students. Since 1971 the teachers have been allowed to construct their own tests.

There appeared to be a high dropout rate for students at about second grade. It seems that once they feel they have achieved literacy or when economic pressures bear down they tend to leave school to enter the working world of adults.

Students were informed by their teachers of their grades and promotion either at the end of the school year or at the beginning of the next. A number of teachers assigned written work, which they graded frequently; this was especially true in the INI schools. Where there is an authoritarian approach, together with a striving for correct answers and little room for dispute, students tend to know when they have answered correctly. Although monthly report cards are required throughout Mexico, only the yearly reports were encounteed in the Highlands. Of course written reports have little or no meaning to illiterate parents. They cannot read, have little idea of what schooling is all about, and often expect their children to repeat a grade several times. Some parents did call on the teachers periodically for more intelligible verbal reports of their children's progress. Generalized reports of school activities were also made at parent meetings, which were held in connection with the two principle school fiestas, Independence and Mother's Days. Teachers reported to their committees whenever called upon to do so; in addition, a committee member was often present in the school to observe the work first hand. Committees dissatisfied with their teachers often have complained to the inspectors in San Cristobal or even to State Directors of Education in the state capital.

With the exception of a few of the normal school graduates, none of the teachers encountered in the field had the educational background to modify the federal curriculum constructively; the normal school teachers, on the other hand, lacked the ability to communicate with their students and, therefore, could make few constructive modifications. Indications of teacher autonomy were found, however, in the common Mexican (and especially Highland Indian) reaction of passivity —avoidance coupled with a show of outward obedience and respect for those of higher authority. This absentee reaction was frequent among most teachers; however, only a few evidenced the interest, character, or educational background that would allow them to function independently. Those who showed the most independence generally did so in community development activities, not in the improvement of the academic curriculum.

THE CHILDREN'S VIEW

The children react to school in a variety of ways. Some attend only because their parents are pressured by tribal authorities into sending them. For example, people are sometimes fined heavily or jailed for a day for keeping their children away. Such children may be very fearful when they do attend and may have little interest in learning what their teachers propose. One woman remembered:

> I wanted to learn a little, but I was afraid. I just cried and cried all day long. The other girls played ball; they were very happy playing with their ball, but I didn't want to touch it. I was afraid of the boys, and the men, and the girls who grabbed me to play with them.

Another young woman, whose parents managed to keep her hidden from the census takers throughout her school years, expressed clearly the conflict between home and school, a conflict that is particularly sharp in the case of young girls, whose modesty and virginity may be threatened by all the contact with unrelated males which school affords:

> I never wanted to go to school, nor did my father want me to go. The girls there have too much to do with men. If I went I would be doing nothing but looking for a husband. I wouldn't learn anything, anyhow. If I went my mother

wouldn't think about me all the time. I would just wander around, enjoying myself, and my parents would be very angry. Perhaps I would be better off learning to read and speak Spanish, but, unfortunately, some of the girls behave poorly there. Not all of them are bad, if they want to behave well they can. They only misbehave if they want to; nobody makes them. Besides, if I went to school I would forget how to work, I would just wander around all day without having anyone tell me what to do.

Virtue was maintained as well as a traditional way of life.

Not all children think ill of school; indeed, it appears that a majority, perhaps more than those who are actually enrolled, do like to attend, especially when they have a good teacher. At school, play is legitimate before and after classes and during recess. In addition, as was shown in Jaime's reading lesson, there is much time for play and socializing during class itself, especially when the teacher is not watching. The opportunity to socialize is much prized by the Indians, most of whom live isolated from one another. They speak of the few inhabited villages and the settlements that have formed around some of the schools as happy places, places where people are not so alone. Children are not alone at school; they are surrounded by playmates. Many of them do look happy at school, especially when playing with one another.

Yet the children feel considerable ambivalence about all the play, for they have already begun to internalize the cultural norm that good children should not waste time in play. Teachers who give little academic work, who appear to take little interest in them, who "let us play all day," are resented; the good child of school age should already be an industrious worker.

Some children like school because it can open horizons beyond their world and can begin to satisfy their curiosity about all that which is not readily known. Many like school because they see a genuine need for speaking Spanish and for at least a smattering of "the three R's."

But more than anything else, the schools have brought at least some children the possibility of an alternative way of life. Before the coming of the schools there was no choice but to follow in one's parents' footsteps, whether one wanted to or not, whether one liked the parent that one was expected to accompany or not. Those children who do not like to farm, who do not like the traditional way of life, or who do not like their parents, see in the schools an opportunity to prepare for a different and better way of life, that of the teacher. This opportunity may be elusory, however, for it is becoming more and more difficult to become a teacher as the number of primary-school graduates skyrockets.[8] But the feeling is very real. One teacher, remembering his own early years, recalled:

When I was a child I wanted to go to school because I didn't like to work around the house or in the milpa. My father tried to hide me every time the teacher came looking for more children for the school, but I went running out so that I would have to go. I wanted to play and to look at the books. Even

---

[8] In 1952, the year the INI opened its first primary schools, no Highland Indians were able to finish primary school, nor were any able to finish for a number of years previous to this. In 1959, the first boys, three in number, were graduated; in 1961, the first girls, also three in number. In 1971 almost 800 were graduated, of whom close to 150 were girls.

when there was no school, when the teacher was away, I hung around the school-house so I wouldn't have to go to the milpa.

When I was in third grade the teacher didn't like me; he wouldn't let me go on to the boarding school in San Cristobal. My heart was very sad.

One day, when I had gone to get firewood with a friend, I said to him, "Look we've flunked. The teacher is going to keep on scolding us, he's going to whip us even harder next year, and then he's going to flunk us all over again. So, let's go to San Cristobal anyway!" But the other boy wasn't interested. I wouldn't give up. One day I told my parents, "I'm going to San Cristobal."

"What are you going to do there?"

"My teacher is taking me. I already told him that I could go."

"How will you go? You're too little to walk all the way." [It takes a man eight hours of hard walking in the dry season, and he was only about ten.]

"Don't worry, I'm going on a horse. (What a lie! I thought.) Don't worry. I'm going."

They gave me some tortillas, some pozol, and 10 pesos to spend. I didn't know what to do; I met some people on the trail, and that's how I got to the school."

[It was days before the entrance exams were held; his money and food ran out, but he was determined to remain. By now his parents had discovered the lie and sent an older brother to bring him home. He begged his brother to let him stay, to see if they would accept him in the school.]

Finally the day of the examination came. I passed. My old teacher was furious. He sent word to the Director of the Boarding School to get rid of me. He said I was irresponsible and should be sent right home. But the Director decided to give me six months as a trial. I stayed in that school for three years, passing every grade. Now I am a teacher.

Other teachers, especially the older ones, tell of being whipped to keep them from school or of being tied to a pole all day, but the determination to prepare for another way of life was great. Many of the younger teachers have not had as hard a psychological struggle to attend school, since the tribal authorities now support them. For example, one youngster enrolled himself in school although he had never been listed by the census takers; every succeeding year he mollified his angry father by explaining that by re-enrolling he had saved him the payment of a heavy fine.

For all but the richest families, however, time spent in school does cut into the children's economic contributions to the family. Attendance is almost always poor, since parents keep their children working as much as possible. This, too, creates ambivalent feelings in many children. One teacher explained.

What can I do when parents come asking permission to keep their children out of school? The other day one father asked for three weeks so he could take his son to a coffee plantation. When I told him that the boy was absent a lot, that he was behind in his studies, the father said, "O.K. And who's going to feed him?" So what could I do?

School and home conflict even though the tribal authorities now tend to give strong support to the schools. The children are caught in the middle. One response is to attend school sporadically, devoting considerable time to home chores. (In 1964 to 1965, attendance averaged slightly over 60 percent.) Another response, as indicated before, is for the children to want their teachers to keep them busy, to keep them too occupied to play. In the children's opinion, this is, perhaps, the most important quality of a teacher, even more important than his ability to explain the work clearly.

When a young child fails to obey his parents' orders he is considered too young to understand; a schoolchild who fails to understand his teacher is considered too stupid. The teacher or a system that offers virtually all instruction in a foreign language is rarely blamed. The teachers, too, reflect this view. Most Indian teachers consider students who fail to learn as lazy or willful. Some blame a child's lack of nutrition for his inability to grasp the schoolwork immediately. When a child has failed to learn a particular lesson it is a rare teacher who feels that it is his responsibility to find another method for presenting the material. Ladino teachers tend, at best, to have a condescending attitude toward their pupils and, at worst, to consider them too stupid to learn anything. Mestizos from out of the area are generally so frustrated by their inability to communicate with their pupils that they give up almost any hope of teaching them anything except by pure rote.

The youngsters are unanimous in their preference for Indian rather than non-Indian teachers. They characterize the mestizo teacher, whether local or not, as interested only in himself, often alcoholic, often absent without cause, and disrespectful of them. His explanations are unclear, he expects little of them in the way of learning, and he punishes readily. Most of the time spent in his class is wasted—in play. Oxchuqueros picture him as being sarcastic, while a group of Tzotziles said he treated them like animals. Poor teachers and ladinos were uniformly identified with one another, even when the same children claimed to be very fond of their current ladino teacher.

The good teacher is uniformly seen as an Indian, for children feel that only an Indian can understand or care about them. He is respectful of his students and caring, a man who works hard, expects a lot of them, and keeps them productively occupied. He also knows how to explain the work clearly, but this is secondary. He may punish (even harshly), use sarcasm, or otherwise embarrass the students, but at least those who continue their schooling beyond the earliest grades see this as serving to spur them on to greater efforts. The productive use of their time is far more important than any temporary discomfort.

Not all children may feel this way about harsh punishments or embarrassment in front of the group. It was not possible to directly question or use projective materials with the younger children, but it may be that harsh treatment is one of the factors influencing children to drop out of school.

None of the children, not even the girls studying at the boarding school in Zinacantan, which was staffed almost entirely by women, was able to picture a woman teacher, good or bad. Indeed, only one female Indian teacher was found to have a woman for her own model; this was a ladina who was particularly kind to her when she first started school.

How do the children see school? There are a great variety of responses. As already mentioned, some see it as a route to an alternative way of life. Others are genuinely interested in learning more than their own community affords. These are the ones most likely to continue their schooling until they finish primary school, despite strong pressures to the contrary from many parents. Many see a need for some knowledge of Spanish and a smattering of "the three Rs" so as to be better able to defend themselves against potential cheating by the ladinos. They can achieve these skills in far less than the six years of formal schooling involved, and generally drop out once they are big enough to make a real contribution to the family's economy, often at about puberty. Others attend school on sufferance and leave as soon as they can. If the schools are truly agencies of acculturation, few children remain in them long enough for many cultural patterns to be changed.[9]

[9] Enrollment figures for the school year 1970–1971 show that less than one percent of school-aged children were enrolled in sixth grade. Although there were almost 800 sixth-graders, almost 3 percent of the 30,000 school-aged children, hardly any of these sixth-graders were young enough (under 15) to be considered of school age.

5 / The effectiveness of the schools

The educational authorities set as their primary goal the incorporation of the children into the national life. How effective were the schools in achieving this goal of acculturation? Despite their almost complete disregard of the local culture, there was one aspect of the program that did take that culture into account, namely the use of the local language for instruction during the earliest grades. What effect did this have? Did it enhance communication between school and community? Did it make the learning of academic material easier, not only during the earlier stages when it was the medium of communication, but also later when Spanish was the only language used? Did it allow the schools to have a greater impact upon their communities?

The questions raised above fall into two areas: One relates to the general impact of the schools on the community, the other to the narrower one of academic achievement. It was possible to gather data relevant to both by comparing several effects of the programs prior to the merger of 1964. Statistical data were used since this allowed more extensive coverage and a larger sample. Replication was used to add to the power of the statistics. The final samples consisted of three tribal areas with a total of twenty-six schools, forty-two teachers, and 1601 children. It was also possible, in a very modest way, to begin to unscramble the relative influences of teachers' ethnicity and the language of instruction.

To measure academic achievement it was decided to concentrate on the one aspect of the curriculum that underlies all others: reading comprehension in the national language (Spanish). The greater a child's reading comprehension in Spanish, the greater his academic advantage; the poorer his comprehension, the greater his handicap. To measure reading comprehension in Spanish a special test was developed, a test that was both appropriate to the children's environment and that exhibited statistical reliability and validity. It was administered in the twenty-six schools to all the children who the teachers felt were able to "understand what they read in Spanish."

To examine the schools' impacts on their communities it was possible to count the number of teacher-initiated development projects, such as the installation of public showers or demonstration farm plots; much of this data appears in Chapter 4. However, another set of measures, reaching into every home (which teacher initiated projects often did not do), was also used; these included data relating to adult literacy and to percentages of school-aged children actually enrolled in school.

NATIONAL OR MOTHER LANGUAGE FOR BEGINNING READING?

The Samples   There were four tribal areas in the Chiapas Highlands at the time of the field study (1964–1965) in which there were a sufficient number of both INI and all-Spanish (federal and state) schools that had been operating long enough to make comparisons of the programs viable; these were Chenalho, Oxchuc, Tenejapa, and Zinacantan. It was decided to work only in schools that had been in continuous operation for at least five years so that long-term effects could be observed. In the end the major testing was done in Oxchuc, the tribe most enthusiastic about schooling, and in Zinacantan, the most resistant. An intermediary tribe was also chosen; while either Tenejapa or Chenalho would have served, the latter was selected because I was already acquainted with it. Thus, school-oriented Oxchuc, intermediary Chenalho, and school-resistant Zinacantan were the three tribes in which major testing was carried out.

It was decided to match hamlets with schools representing the two approaches within each tribal area rather than to match individual children; it was not possible to confide in any of the more traditional measures used to match subjects in

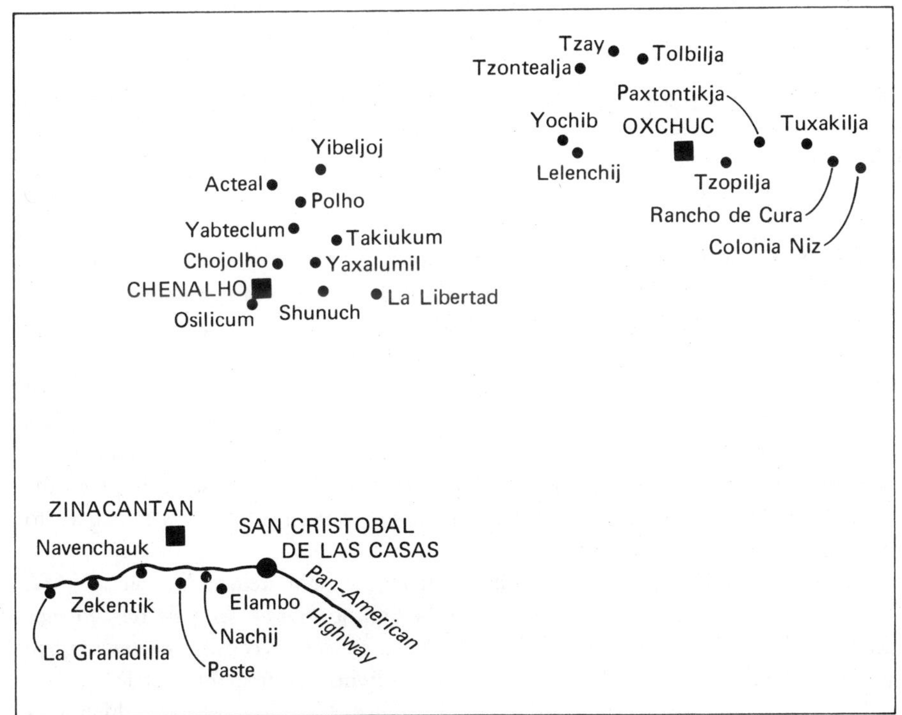

Schools visited during the course of the reading study.

educational experiments, such as IQs, aptitude tests, or even chronological ages as reported by the children (they had little notion of their chronological ages). Moreover, it was felt that since universal schooling was all but unknown in the local communities, the school might be exerting selective pressures for attendance and that percentages of enrollment and attendance could serve as measures of school–community relations. Thus whole communities were matched.

There is some discussion within the anthropological literature to indicate that there may be subtle cultural differences among the various hamlets of a given tribal area (for example, see Nash 1970; Vogt 1969), but these variations have almost always been described in terms of differential participation in tribal leadership or dialect differences; significant differences in patterns of child rearing or education have not come to light as yet. Despite this, an effort was made to match the schools' communities, one by one within each municipio, pairing INI and all-Spanish school districts.

The procedures used to select the actual schools in which the testing was to be done varied from one municipio to another. In Chenalho there were six INI and eight federal or state schools in operation. It was decided to test in those that both were located nearest to the ceremonial center (*cabezera*) and where there were fewest children from other tribes enrolled.

In order to select the schools in Oxchuc, where there were over twenty schools in operation at the time, the municipal President was interviewed regarding the economic, health, and religious characteristics of each of the hamlets that maintained schools; based on his descriptions five INI and five federal schools were selected. In Zinacantan only three INI schools had been in continuous operation for more than five years; all were located near the Pan American Highway. Three state schools located near the Highway were matched with them. In all, twenty-six schools were selected for testing, ten each in Chenalho and Oxchuc, and six in Zinacantan. Within each municipio half of the selected schools had been using the INI's bilingual approach all along, and half the all-Spanish approach of the state and federal schools.

Data was gathered regarding the overall economy, health, and religious practices of each community. As can be seen from Table 1, both sets of communities within each municipio resembled each other considerably.

Development of the Reading Test   The reading comprehension test was developed during a series of pilot studies conducted from 1959 to 1963 in six tribal areas. It was felt that the test, in addition to demonstrating traditional measures of validity and reliability, had to relate to the children's real world and had to use a testing format that they could easily understand. Since no tests existed at the time of the field study that fulfilled all of these requirements it was necessary to develop one.

In its final form the group test consists of eighty-eight items (Modiano 1966a, 1966b). Sample items are included at the beginning of two sections but are not set apart from the material to be scored. The first section consists of twenty-five multiple-choice picture-identification vocabulary items, the first three of them used only for training; all correct responses are nouns. The next section, which is a continuation of the first, consists of fifteen multiple-choice phrase-reading items in which only the verbs change. The third section is composed of twelve items that call for the following of one-phrase directions. The remainder of the test consists of paragraph interpretation. There are nine stories, the first two serving for training. Each paragraph is accompanied by an average of four sentences that must be marked yes or no (true or false); of the thirty sentences to be graded, twenty-two repeat the words in the main paragraph, four use synonyms, and four call for inferences.

The test was first administered in its final form in the ten Chenalho schools. The correlation between these test scores and teachers' estimates of their pupils' reading ability was only .443 ($N = 84$). Although this correlation is significant ($p < .001$), it was decided to obtain additional measures of reading comprehension in Spanish to demonstrate the statistical validity of the test. One such method was comparison with students' scores on the five-item reading-comprehension section of the yearly promotional examination. In addition, an individualized test of Spanish reading-comprehension was developed.

The individualized test was first pilot-tested with eighty-four students at the semiboarding school of Chamula, where there was a sufficient number of students in the upper grades to permit evaluation of the upper ranges of the test. The correlation between the individualized and the group tests for grades one to five was .748 ($N = 77$). This is considerably higher than many of the correlations used to demonstrate the validity of our most popular standardized reading-comprehension tests.

Testing was not repeated in Chenalho, but the individualized test was added to the test battery in Oxchuc and Zinacantan.

Gathering of the Data on Reading Comprehension Since the environment in which the testing was done is considerably different from that encountered in the United States, it may be appropriate to include at this point, for North American educators unaccustomed to field conditions, a somewhat more detailed description of the testing situation than would normally be done for an educational evaluation or for anthropologists.

My Indian assistant and I traveled by horse and by foot, with one or more pack animals, in the company of one or more guides (often children who took us from their school to the next one). Upon arriving at a school I would present the credentials supplied by the Inspector of the Zone to the Director and would be given a space, often at the back of the classroom, where we would camp. After recess or the next morning the teacher would make some introductory remarks to his students, in Spanish, Tzotzil, or Tzeltal, as he wished. I would follow, speaking in Spanish, telling the children that they should not be afraid, that this was a study comparing many schools, that they should try to do their best, but that they would in no way be penalized for the test (*prueba*) results. My assistant immediately translated this into the local language.

In order to help the children become somewhat accustomed to me, to my assistant, and to the testing situation, three drawing tests were first administered, followed by the group test of reading comprehension and, in Oxchuc and Zinacantan, by the individualized tests. We remained in the community for two to five consecutive school days, depending on the number of children tested individually.

TABLE 1 DEMOGRAPHIC DATA FOR THE HAMLETS SERVED BY THE SAMPLE SCHOOLS*

Tribal Area (Municipio) School System	Hamlet (Paraje)	Population	Climate[1]	Diet[2]	Health[3]	Outside Contacts[4]	Principal Sources of Income[5]	Proportion of Catholics
Chenalho								
Federal	Acteal	500	T	A	A	1	A	1.00
	La Libertad	326	T	A	A	1	B	1.00
	Yabteclum	1099	T	A	A	1	A	1.00
State	Chojolho	217	T	A	A	2	CE	1.00
	Osilicum	350	T	A	A	2	A	1.00
Institute	Polho	550	T	A	A	1	A	1.00
	Shunuch	365	T	A	A	2	B	.80
	Takiukum	565	T	A	A	1	A	1.00
	Yaxalumil	204	T	A	A	1	A	1.00
	Yibeljoj	400	T	A	A	1	A	1.00
Oxchuc								
Federal	Lelenchij	563	C	A	A	2	BD	.90
	Colonia Niz	776	C	A	A	3	BD	.95
	Rancho de Cura	570	C	A	A	2	BCG	.50
	Tzay	647	T	B	A	3	AB	.50
	Yochib	890	T	B	A	3	AB	.60
Institute	Paxtontikja	600	T	A	A	2	AB	.20
	Tolbilja	620	T	B	A	2	ABD	.50
	Tuxakilja	554	C	A	A	2	AB	.70
	Tzontealja	675	T	B	A	1	AB	.50
	Tzopilja	759	C	A	A	2	ABC	.85

TABLE 1 (*continued*)

Tribal Area (Municipio) School System	Hamlet (Paraje)	Population	Climate[1]	Diet[2]	Health[3]	Outside Contacts[4]	Principal Sources of Income[5]	Proportion of Catholics
Zinacantan								
State	Nachij	900	C	A	P	3	AB	1.00
	Navenchauc	4025	C	A	A	4	AF	1.00
	Zekentik	275	C	A	A	3	C	1.00
Institute	Elambo	511	C	A	A	3	AC	1.00
	La Granadilla	458	T	A	A	3	AC	1.00
	Paste	1247	C	A	B	3	A	1.00

[1] Climate at the school house
T = Temperate (up to 6000 feet above sea level)
C = cold (above 6000 feet)

[2] A = average (corn, beans, chile, vegetable greens, little fruit)
B = better (all of the above, plus tropical fruits in season)

[3] Based on frequency of contacts with medical help including native healers, estimates of infant mortality, and estimated average age of adult deaths
A = average
B = better
P = poorer

[4] 1 = little (no *mestizos* in residence; men visit San Cristobal an average of up to four times yearly)
2 = some (*mestizos* visit the hamlet and live nearby; men visit San Cristobal up to twice monthly)
3 = frequent (same as above, but men visit San Cristobal up to twice weekly)
4 = constant (almost daily contact with *mestizos*)

[5] A = sale of crops
B = plantation labor
C = local day labor
D = small scale aviculture
E = small scale animal husbandry
F = small scale commerce
G = alleged remnants of serfdom (*baldaje*)

* SOURCE: Nancy Modiano, "Bilingual Education for Children of Linguistic Minorities," *America Indigena* 28, No. 2 (México, D. F.: Institúto Indigenista Interamericano, 1968), pp. 405–414.

The purpose of the drawing tests was not to obtain data for equating populations, as would be done in the United States, but merely to provide a buffer experience during which we hoped that the children would lose some of their fearfulness, learn that my assistant and I could be depended upon for help and direction, become accustomed to responding to our slightly different speech patterns (in Spanish and, for my assistant, in the local language), and become acquainted with our testing procedures.

The first buffer tests consisted of the Bender-Gestalt (Bender 1946) and the House–Tree–Two Person–Animal set (Buck 1948; Schwartz and Rosenberg 1955). They were administered to entire classroom groups; an effort was made to test all the children in attendance. I gave all instructions in Spanish and my assistant immediately translated them into the local language. As the children began to draw we walked around the room encouraging and praising.

The Frostig Test   In some of the schools (an equal number for each approach within each tribe) the teacher was then asked to excuse the beginners from further testing. The remaining children were given the Frostig Developmental Test of Visual Perception (Frostig 1961). The children whose teachers considered that they could read ($N = 59$) and who demonstrated that ability to at least some degree on

Children taking the Bender-Gestalt, Chenalho.

the tests of reading comprehension averaged a Mental Age of only 5.8 on the Frostig subtest dealing with position in space (reversals and rotations) and only 6.6 and 6.9, respectively, on shape constancy and spatial relations.

Frostig developed her norms (1962) on 1825 children aged three to nine in eleven California communities, and they appear to be carefully developed and valid for the population studied. There is an interesting discrepancy, however, between the results of the Chiapas and California groups, especially in the subtest on which the Chiapas children scored poorest. The subtest of position in space involves the reversals and rotations of simple line drawings resembling "common" objects presented in series. It is generally believed in the United States that similar discriminations must be made in distinguishing, for example, the letters *b, d, p,* and *q.* The children had relatively little difficulty with the highly stylized and simplified table, chair, moon, or flower drawings but considerable difficulty with the doll and the cube; hardly any were able to handle the ladder or the beach ball successfully. In the shape constancy test they were easily distracted by irrelevant shapes, and for spatial relations they were able to reproduce the drawings globally but were not sufficiently accurate on the more detailed ones to receive credit.

What emerges from these tests is that, since all fifty-nine children could, in fact, read, the content of the tests may be less related to the act of reading than has previously been assumed. The selected children were able to distinguish

Children taking the Bender-Gestalt, Chenalho.

b-d-p-q-g, and *h-m-n-ñ-r*, and similar combinations; they were able to isolate words within a paragraph and letters within a word, in order to read them; and they were able to distinguish and correctly reproduce words that look like one another. Moreover, they were able to do this in a half-understood language. Poor as the quality of instruction may have been for many, it was sufficient to enable them to learn to read. They had been instructed solely in the shapes of letters and in their associated sounds. They had not been instructed with the plethora of picture-interpretation activities generally deemed essential to the teaching of reading in the United States; thus their picture interpretation skills were not as well developed as is generally true in the United States. It appears, as a result of this study, that many reading-readiness activities may not be as directly related to the acquisition of reading skills as has heretofore been believed.

Administration of the Reading Tests   After the Bender-Gestalt and H–T–TP–A were administered the teacher was asked to indicate which students were able to ". . . understand what they read in Spanish," for further testing. These students were counted, as were those who had not been selected. The proportions of students selected for further testing were computed by approach (all-Spanish or bilingual) for each tribe; the comparisons of these proportions became one of the key statistics used in evaluating the two approaches.

The selected students were first given the Frostig test in some of the schools and then administered the NYDO (Maccoby 1958) in all of them; these were the last of the buffer tests. On the left-hand side of each of four pages of the NYDO is a drawing (leaf, flower, fish, duck); above each drawing is written, "This is a. . . . [name of object]." I read the sentences aloud to the children and encouraged them to read aloud along with me. From this point on test directions were given in Spanish only.

As the children finished they were offered a rest period, but they often asked to continue. I took this as an indication that the buffer tests had served their purpose and that the children had become somewhat accustomed to the testing situation, my assistant, and myself. Since then I have come to realize that in a number of schools my visit provided one of the few occasions devoted to intensive academic-like work, where considerable effort was made to assure the students' understanding of what was expected of them. In any event they appeared to be enjoying themselves and often asked to continue rather than to rest.

The group test of reading comprehension in Spanish was now administered. The first three picture–vocabulary items were carefully demonstrated, using a combination of the test booklet and the blackboard. The students were encouraged to participate actively in supplying correct answers. Every paper was carefully checked to make sure that the directions had been followed. They were then told to complete all the picture items and, as each finished, to answer the twelve questions on the page following the omitted antonyms. After a short break the remainder of the test was demonstrated and then completed by the children. Following the completion of the group test the children in Oxchuc and Zinacantan were called outside one by one for the individualized test.

Results and Discussion   Two principal measures were used to determine the relative effectiveness of the all-Spanish and bilingual approaches for reading comprehension in Spanish. One was the comparison of proportions of students chosen by their teachers as able to ". . . understand what they read in Spanish." In all three municipios the proportions favored the bilingual INI schools; when the probabilities are combined they are significant at beyond the .001 level (see Table 2). It may have been that the Institute teachers were more lenient than the others in making their selections.

TABLE 2   PROPORTIONS OF STUDENTS SELECTED BY THEIR TEACHERS AS
". . . ABLE TO UNDERSTAND WHAT THEY READ IN SPANISH"*

Language of Initial Reading Instruction	Chenalho	Oxchuc	Zinacantan
National Language (Federal and State Schools)			
Selected	66	54	45
Not Selected	227	313	107
Total Attendance	293	367	152
Proportion Selected	.225	.147	.296
Mother Language (Institute Schools)			
Selected	49	187	54
Not Selected	150	273	76
Total Attendance	199	460	130
Proportion Selected	.246	.407	.415
Total			
Selected	115	241	99
Not Selected	337	586	183
Total Attendance	492	827	282
Proportion Selected	.234	.291	.351
Chi-square (d.f. = 1) Combined $p < .001$	.216	66.512	1.331

* SOURCE: Nancy Modiano, "Bilingual Education for Children of Linguistic Minorities," *America Indigena* 28, No. 2 (México, D.F.: Institúto Indigenista Interamericano, 1968), pp. 405–414.

The second principal measure was the scores on the group test. Again, the INI schools averaged higher than the others in all three municipios, giving a combined probability of beyond the .001 level (see Table 3).

On the basis of these results, it would appear that the INI teachers were even more stringent in their criteria of "able to understand" than were the monolingual-approach teachers. More importantly, both measures showed the bilingual approach to be significantly more effective in teaching reading comprehension in Spanish.

Why is it that the bilingual INI schools were more successful in teaching reading comprehension in Spanish? The debate over the bilingual approach and the exclusive use of the national language for the schooling of linguistic minorities has waxed and waned over the years, the arguments often being based more on emotion and prejudice than on empirical evidence.

TABLE 3   DISTRIBUTION OF SCORES ON THE GROUP READING TEST*

Language of Initial Reading Instruction	Chenalho	Oxchuc	Zinacantan
National Language (Federal and State Schools)			
Mean	32.91	47.20	47.60
SD	20.85	16.81	14.98
Range	0–81	14–75	19–76
Median	26.50	47.83	50.00
Number	66	54	45
Mother Language (Institute Schools)			
Mean	46.14	50.75	52.52
SD	14.89	18.42	22.28
Range	14–73	2–84	0–84
Median	47.74	60.25	60.83
Number	49	187	54
Total			
Mean	38.55	49.96	50.28
SD	19.67	18.13	19.46
Range	0–81	2–84	0–84
Median	30.20	41.52	52.15
Number	115	241	99
t	3.86	1.26	1.25
$(d.f. = 1)$			
Combined $p < .001$			

* SOURCE: Nancy Modiano, "Bilingual Education for Children of Linguistic Minorities," *America Indigena* 28, No. 2 (México, D.F.: Institúto Indigenista Interamericano, 1968), pp. 405–414.

The few comparative studies that have been conducted have all shown results favoring the bilingual approach. Evaluative studies of bilingual education have come primarily from the Soviet Union, where authors such as Kreusler (1961) and Serduchenko (1962) have juxtaposed the use of the mother tongue in formal schooling with the rapid spread of literacy during the years following the Revolution of 1917.

Other studies come from diverse parts of the world. Malherbe (1943) showed that the language of both Afrikaans- and English-speaking students was enhanced by a bilingual approach; he did not concern himself with the education of the much larger aboriginal population, however. Fife and Manuel (1951) showed that the use of English as the medium of instruction in Puerto Rico hampered achievement in other academic areas and suggested that its introduction should be delayed until fourth grade, by which time most children attending school would have dropped out. In Ghana, Grieve and Taylor (1952) found that the use of the vernacular proved more effective than the use of English, although they complained that the statistics they reported were questionable because of unmatched groups and teachers unsophisticated in research techniques. Several Mexican authors (for example, Barrera-Vazquez 1953; Castro 1959; de la Fuente 1940) found that bilingual programs proved to be more popular and therefore more successful than the all-Spanish programs which had preceded them.

The first major comparative study of bilingual education to rely upon statistical data was conducted in the Philippines (Orata 1953). It showed that the children in the bilingual group, who received all instruction in Hiligaynon, except for English as a second language, had higher levels of achievement in all academic areas, including reading, both before and after the third year, when English became the medium of instruction and testing, than did those in the all-English group. The experimental (bilingual approach) children were also reported to have more positive feelings for school, more carry-over of academic activities into nonschool life, and higher cognitive levels. It is unfortunate that no efforts were made to counteract the halo effect and that the statistical data was reported sketchily. The results of comparative studies based upon newly popular bilingual education in the U.S.A. have yet to be disseminated.

Proponents of the monolingual approach (the teaching of reading exclusively in the national language) have always recognized the need for the student to understand the national language in order to read it with comprehension. They advocate prior or simultaneous oral instruction in the second language and in the reading of it. For example, both Tireman (1948) and Morrison (1958), in reviewing the situation then prevalent for Spanish-speaking children in New Mexico and in New York City respectively, stressed that the development of an English vocabulary was essential prior to the achievement of reading comprehension. They devoted the bulk of their reports to suggestions for improving instruction in English as a second language.

When the language is understood a number of factors then enter into reading comprehension. Various authors describe them differently, but factor analytic studies have all revealed two major factors: vocabulary, which accounts for about 50 percent of the variation, and a second factor that appears to be some aspect of verbal reasoning based on a thorough mastery of the grammar (for example, see Anderson 1949; Davis 1944, 1956; Langsam 1941; Hall and Robinson 1945; Jan-Tausch 1962; Holmes 1954).

A number of additional factors affect reading comprehension, some including the reader's purpose, his experience with the language, his perception of the graphic symbols and their legibility, his experience with the concepts the author is trying to convey, as well as the style in which the material is written. In addition, both the reader's physical condition and his physical and social environment affect comprehension.

There is evidence that reading involves much the same processes in all languages, regardless of whether they are transcribed in any of the alphabets, syllabaries, or ideographs now in use throughout the world. Gray (1956), in a study of seventy-eight adults reading in fourteen languages that included a wide variety of writing systems, demonstrated that both the physical act of reading and the process of comprehension are much the same for mature readers regardless of language or representative style.

The relation, however, between knowledge of a language and the acquisition of skills for decoding and word recognition has not been the center of much scholarly inquiry. That people's perception of graphic symbols is strongly influenced both by their experience and by the meaning they can give to the symbol has been demonstrated by Piaget and Inhelder (1969), as well as by others (for example, see Bruner 1957, 1958; Segal, Campbell, and Herskovitz 1966). It has also been demonstrated that people have trouble recognizing words with which they are unfamiliar, just as they often fail to recognize phonemic contrasts (see, for example, Bloomfield 1933; Boaz 1889; Brière 1966; Lado 1957; Sapir 1925; Weinreich 1953; Wolff 1950).

Thus not only does the child who is learning to read in a foreign language have trouble understanding what he is supposed to read, but his very perception of the graphic symbols and his ability to associate them with recognizable utterances are drastically affected. This kind of reading becomes far more frustrating than learning to decipher material which is potentially significant. It is much easier and less confusing to learn to read material that is intrinsically meaningful than material which is essentially incomprehensible.

Considering the high level of frustration involved in such activity, it is small wonder that the bilingual INI schools were more appealing to their students than were the others.

Beyond the use of the mother tongue for beginning reading, another feature of the INI curriculum that differed from that of the all-Spanish program was the role given to formal instruction in the national language. In the federal and state schools Spanish was the medium of instruction, but instruction in Spanish as a second language was virtually nonexistent. Rather, it was expected that by using only Spanish the children would somehow acquire a working knowledge of that language. Such an assumption has been invoked time and time again, throughout the world, yet no research has proven its validity. In the INI schools some consistent attention was given to formal instruction in Spanish as a second language; however scanty it may have been, it was more than what was offered under the all-Spanish approach. The children in the INI schools enjoyed two advantages in learning to read Spanish: (1) They learned to decode on potentially meaningful material, and (2) they received some aid in learning Spanish. By the time they began to read Spanish they already knew how to decode and they had some knowledge of that langauge.

SCHOOL–COMMUNITY RELATIONS

Ever since the founding of the first *Casa del Pueblo* (House of the People) in the 1920s, Mexico has considered the rural schools as community centers and development agencies as much as centers for academic instruction. The INI gave added emphasis to this policy in the schools it founded. Yet there is a counter-current, coming primarily from the teachers' union and the normal schools, that identifies the teacher's function primarily as being one of academic instruction. What impact do the schools have on the Indian communities they serve? Was there any difference between effectiveness of the INI and the all-Spanish (federal and state) schools?

All the schools are supposed to sponsor community development programs at the local level. These programs can include agricultural and animal husbandry demonstrations, health services, improved communication and transportation, and other forms of economic improvement. In the twenty-six sample schools a number of these teacher-initiated projects were encountered. Two state schools in Zinacantan had flower gardens bordering their buildings; people have been growing flowers commercially for many years in Zinacantan and the schools may have introduced new varieties. (It was not possible to determine whether the impetus for these gardens came directly from the teachers or from other sources.) Many of the schools, both federal and INI, had agricultural demonstration plots; most were located in INI schools. Two federal schools were located near the sites of large, old, and established Sunday markets; it was not possible, again, to determine whether or not these markets had originally been founded by teachers. At the time of the study two INI schools had just begun local Saturday markets; both were located hours away from any major (Sunday) market. Most other community improvement projects encountered were found at INI schools. These included four classes in the use of the sewing machine (three in INI schools, one in a federal school), four public showers (three in INI schools, one in a federal school), and two public laundries, both in INI schools. Thus it appears that more community development projects emanated from INI than from state or federal schools.

Other measures of the schools' effectiveness in their communities (in terms of the area's total population) also favored INI schools. These included proportions of literate adults in the area served by each school, proportions of area populations enrolled in school, female proportions of school enrollment, and female proportions of students selected for testing. All were significant, with probabilities combined, at beyond the .001 level (see Table 4).

The last two statistics, the proportions of girls enrolled in the schools and the proportions who had succeeded in their studies well enough for their teachers to consider them able to understand what they read in Spanish, reflect some of the more subtle aspects of the school's relation to its community. The teachers are almost always men, and boys and girls sit in the same classrooms. Both conditions conflict with the local culture, which encourages the separation of the sexes once children reach working and school age. Many parents oppose sending their girls to school even more than their boys, since the girls will be exposed to the company of many boys and will probably work with a man who is unrelated to them (stories of male teachers forcing themselves upon nubile girls were rare but not unknown). Moreover, it is felt that men will have greater use of literacy in their dealings with ladinos than will women. Thus the extent to which the schools were able to attract girls and work with them effectively indicates the confidence the communities felt in their teachers. Again, it was the INI schools, with their fuller recognition of the local culture and with their Indian teachers, that were more successful.

TEACHERS' ETHNICITY

Confounded in all of the data comparing the effectiveness of the INI and the federal or state schools has been the teachers' ethnicity. The INI schools were taught by Indians, the other schools by outsiders. Was it really the differences in school programs that caused the greater effectiveness of the INI schools, or was it the fact that the teachers were themselves Indians? As was pointed out in Chapter 4, the children felt far more confidence and acceptance with Indian teachers than with outsiders, whether they were local ladinos or mestizos from other parts of Mexico.

TABLE 4   DIFFERENCES BETWEEN NATIONAL (FEDERAL AND STATE) AND MOTHER LANGUAGE (INI) SCHOOLS*

Tribal Area	Adult Literacy[1]	Enroll-ment[2]	Female Enroll-ment[3]	Girls Selected for Testing[4]
Chenalho				
National Language	.054	.169	.269	.065
Mother Language	.076	.178	.249	.200
Total	.064	.173	.259	.124
Chi-Square	9.231	.664	.426	5.660
Oxchuc				
National Language	.046	.152	.357	.017
Mother Language	.061	.206	.371	.234
Total	.053	.178	.365	.146
Chi-Square	6.778	38.081	.240	26.218
Zinacantan				
National Language	.016	.075	.148	.000
Mother Language	.029	.118	.395	.308
Total	.019	.086	.247	.193
Chi-Square	16.030	35.962	51.060	11.816
Combined p	<.001	<.001	<.001	<.001

[1] Adult Literacy = $\dfrac{\text{literate adults}}{\text{total hamlet population of selected schools}}$

[2] Enrollment = $\dfrac{\text{total school enrollment}}{\text{total hamlet population of selected schools}}$

[3] Female Enrollment = $\dfrac{\text{female enrollment}}{\text{total enrollment}}$

[4] Girls Selected for Testing = $\dfrac{\text{girls selected for testing}}{\text{female attendance}}$

* SOURCE: Nancy Modiano, "Bilingual Education for Children of Linguistic Minorities," *America Indigena* 28, No. 2 (México, D.F.: Instituto Indigenista Interamericano, 1968), pp. 405–414.

It was possible during the school visits to begin to separate the teachers' ethnicity from the effectiveness of the program, although the sample was so small (only two Indian teachers worked in state schools) that no definitive conclusions can be drawn. (At the time of the field survey no ladinos used the local language in their teaching, although some have since begun to do so.)

The two Indian teachers in question were reputed to be neither the very best nor the very worst of the teachers; one held considerable sway in his community, but the other was poorly regarded. The students of these teachers, who taught exclusively in Spanish, did score higher on the group reading test than did those of the mestizo teachers working with the same tribe (Chenalho), although the difference is not statistically significant; the students in the INI schools, however, scored significantly higher (see Table 5). Thus, the two Indian teachers working exclusively in Spanish were more successful academically than were their mestizo counterparts, but not as successful as other Indians working with the bilingual program. Similar differences were noted in the data related to school–community contacts.

TABLE 5   DIFFERENCES ON THE GROUP READING TEST AMONG STUDENTS OF MESTIZOS WHO TAUGHT BEGINNING READING IN SPANISH, INDIANS WHO TAUGHT BEGINNING READING IN SPANISH, AND INDIANS WHO TAUGHT BEGINNING READING IN TZOTZIL

	I Mestizo	II Indian	III Indian
Teachers *N*	(3)	(2)	(8)
Language of Initial *Reading Instruction*	Spanish	Spanish	Tzotzil
Mean	28.85	35.55	46.14
SD	28.913	22.602	14.887
Range	2–65	0–81	14–73
Median	26.17	29.50	47.75
N	26	40	49
t		1.626	2.621
p		NS	$<.05$

A sample of only two teachers is too small to offer anything approaching definitive proof, especially in the absence of replication, but it can serve to indicate direction. From this small sample it appears not only that Indian teachers were able to work more effectively than mestizos, but that the bilingual approach added considerably to their effectiveness.

The relation between the teachers' ethnicity and their effectiveness in the Chiapas Indian schools throws light on what is a universal problem in the development of educational systems. Staffing for mass education is highly responsive to economic restraints, directly affecting the number of teaching positions, salaries, and funds for the training of teachers. There are also historical and social constraints that affect the pool from which potential teachers are drawn. In a land in which only the elite receive formal education there are very few potential teachers for mass education. A few countries choose to expand the educational system very slowly while staffing it with highly trained teachers, but most developing nations choose to expand the system rapidly by using poorly trained teachers. Both approaches have been used in Chiapas; normal school graduates have been imported from out of the region to staff some schools, and local Indians, themselves sometimes barely literate when they began teaching, have been assigned to other schools. It appeared that the poorly trained teachers who were members of the local tribes were more successful both academically and in their community development activities than were the more highly trained outsiders.

THE EFFECTIVENESS OF THE SCHOOLS

How effective are the Indian schools of the Chiapas Highlands, and effective according to whose standards—the Indians' or the schools'?

The avowed purpose of the schools is to Mexicanize the Indians, to bring them into the mainstream of national life. In prevailing Highland terms this means giving them the ladino orientation and sense of identification with Mexican life. It also means giving them some ladino skills for relating effectively to the national culture. Especially stressed are skills for communicating in Spanish both orally and in writing.

How do the Indians respond to these efforts? To what extent does their point of view differ from that of the ladinos? Economically a symbiotic relationship exists, with Indians supplying manual labor and ladinos supplying money and goods brought in from the outside; socially and politically, however, almost no relationship exists. Indian children are reared to do manual work and to take pride in their ability to work hard. The training may at times be harsh, but it is felt that only through eagerness to work hard can one hope to survive in the uncertain world in which he lives. It is a world in which much is unknown, where the ladinos command, and where scarcity prevails.

Many say the Indians are eager to change their relationship with the outside world. They want to know more about it and to understand it better. They want to be the masters of their own fates, at least as much as their gods will permit, rather than always depend upon the whims of the ladinos. Theirs is a limited world in which almost all resources are now being used and which has little room for expansion. Indeed, in many of the tribes men must look beyond the municipio for much of their income, and, especially among the Tzeltals, emigration is becoming increasingly common. Lowered mortality rates and rising population constantly increase the economic pressures.

But curiosity about the bigger world is not limited to the economic sphere. Alternative explanations about natural phenomena are sought, and, as it becomes available, modern medicine is increasingly adopted. Some Indians are even prepared to change their religion; Protestant missionaries have found fertile soil, especially among the Tzeltals, and some others have exchanged pantheistic practices for Roman Catholic ceremonies. In Oxchuc few now practice the old Mayan rituals.

Children are given more freedom than adults to satisfy their curiosity about the world. Their play is largely unsupervised and not seriously curtailed until the eve of adolescence, allowing them ample opportunity to explore their environment and to come to terms with adult culture through imitative play. Almost no attempts are made to stifle their curiosity; it is the children rather than the adults who can observe strangers and strange phenomena freely and ask myriad questions. Childhood is truly an age of exploration.

But while children's exploratory activities are largely unsupervised, they are carefully inducted into the world of adult work and allowed to participate at least on the fringe in all other adult activities. The assumption is that if a child is exposed often enough to situations that require understanding but no special skills, such as participation in many religious activities, he will in time become accustomed to the situation and to his role in it. Similarly, where skill learning is involved the child is encouraged to practice the new skill, always to some practical end, and to gradually build his mastery of it until he attains full adult competence, until he becomes so accustomed to it that he can work without striving to remember the various steps. But the skill is never practiced in the abstract; rather it is learned as a part of the family's working activities. Thus a girl learns to make tortillas by helping her mother prepare them. At first her tortillas come out so poorly that they are only good for animals, but with more practice they form the core of first the girl's, and then the family's, diet. A boy learns to farm by first helping his father with a miniature hoe, but he tires easily and starts playing. Although his father may call him back to the task several times, he accomplishes very little. With time and practice, always in the family's milpa or at a job where his father is being paid, he begins to distinguish the weeds from the edible plants and to spend less time in play. With even more practice he becomes accustomed to the work and begins to manage a milpa for himself.

Two factors stand out in the Indian style of education: (1) With sufficient practice at tasks that are an intrinsic part of the family's activities, the child is expected to become accustomed to his work, and (2) children are given considerable leeway, even encouragement, to explore the world around them. This is as true for girls as for boys, although the work they learn to perform is often quite different, and although many adult activities are strongly sex-typed.

This attitude toward education contrasts strongly with ladino styles of child rearing and education, especially for those above the lowest rungs of the socioeconomic scale. Teachers, as members of the upper-middle stratum of the ladino world, distinguish many childhood activities from adult ones and expect children to learn from intrinsically meaningless tasks and to enjoy their rewards in the vague future of adulthood. Like the Indians, the ladinos tend to include children in many adult activities, at least as passive observers, but, unlike the Indians, a child's first efforts at a difficult task are likely to be discarded as worthless. It is only after he has reached a level of proficiency approximating adult skill that his work will be valued by the family. Thus a girl learning to embroider is likely to see all her first attempts used as rags or as dolls' clothing; once she can embroider fairly well her work may be framed or used to adorn a pillow on the living room couch.

All ladinos except the very poorest (who are barely acculturated Indians themselves in many cases) expect their children to attend school, the number of years and particular school varying according to the family's position on the social scale. Their expectation is for school work to be largely rote, intrinsically meaningless and boring, although the rewards of formal education are considered to be sufficiently great at adulthood to warrant the unpleasant aspects of school life. Moreover there is always recess and dismissal times with their rich social life for the children to enjoy. For themselves the ladinos see schooling as an essential experience in the process of becoming an adult, an experience that will give the child the necessary tools, such as literacy, arithmetic, and diplomas, for economic and social success.

The Indians see the schools in quite a different light. They feel themselves greatly disadvantaged in their dealings with ladinos and see formal education as offering some skills with which they can better defend themselves. Indeed, self-defense is the almost universally given response to questions regarding the value of schooling. It is felt that this self-defense is best gained through a working knowledge of the Spanish language and through some literacy. However, the need for literacy is so limited in Indian communities that the average man need not know much more than how to sign his name; women seldom need to do even that. The ability to read and understand the documents one has to sign, as is occasionally required by the municipal authorities, would also be helpful, as would the ability to correspond with family members away at the coffee plantations or to read the labels on patent medicines. Protestantism also encourages its members to read religious tracts, usually written in Tzeltal or Tzotzil. But beyond this, literacy has no function in people's lives. Although they seldom mention it, a knowledge of simple arithmetic is also desirable so that marriage payments can be kept track of and so that people can make sure that the ladino merchants give them their correct change in all transactions. Nothing else that the school may teach is seen as particularly helpful, although it is nice to know more about the larger world. Balanced against the desirability of limited literacy and a knowledge of Spanish are strong feelings against the mixing of boys and girls in the same classroom, sending girls to work with nonrelated male teachers, and the absenting of all children from their household chores. Many a parent has said, in effect, "As long as I keep my child in school he can't learn what is really important."

While the Indians remain ambivalent about the values of schooling, the educational authorities wish to enroll all the children they can find and to Mexicanize them. A knowledge of Spanish and literacy are seen as first steps in this process. Equally important is inculcating in each child a sense of identification with and love for his country. They encourage the children, whether directly or unconsciously, to acculturate to the point of abandoning their home culture whether or not they eventually leave the community physically. Many mestizo teachers, whether local ladinos or not, disparage the local language and encourage their students to change their language along with their clothing. Having changed his language and his clothing, the child has become a little ladino who can be expected to move into the ladino culture during adolescence. This is considered to be the apex of success by many ladino teachers. Indian teachers tend to feel more ambivalent about the purposes of schooling.

To what extent do the schools succeed at their avowed aims? Before they can proceed toward the accomplishment of their goals they must get the children into the school buildings. As we have seen, enrollment varies considerably from one tribe to another. From recent visits I have gathered the impression that, in Oxchuc at least, all the boys and almost all the girls are now enrolled in school for a few years. Very few go beyond first or second grade, but from this generation on at least rudimentary Spanish and literacy can be expected of all Oxchuqueros. At the other extreme is the case of Chamula, where many parents still hide their children from the census takers so as to keep them off the school rolls and where most children, especially the girls, do not attend school.

Once enrolled in school, children's attendance also varies, although here it appears to be at least as much a function of teacher-community relations as of a more generalized opposition to schooling. Teachers who are often absent, abusive, drunk, or ineffective, are likely to have poorer attendance than those who are sober, conscientious, considerate, and effective in the classroom. The membership of the parents' committees also plays a part in attendance, with committee members who are vitally concerned about the functioning of the school being far more effective in rounding up the children than those who resent their committee assignments and who try to pass their year in office with as little effort as possible.

Once the children are enrolled and attending, there is considerable concurrence between what the Indians and the school authorities want for them, at least during the earliest grades. Both want the children to learn Spanish, to read and write, and to learn some elementary arithmetic. Little wonder, then, that enrollment and attendance are strongest in the first few grades. Few Indians seem to want anything more of the schools and most children drop out once they have acquired the rudiments of the three R's and Spanish.

But the schools want far more for the children. They want to Mexicanize them. They want to acculturate them. Beyond the Spanish and the literacy they give much weight to patriotic symbols and ceremonies. Since these are seldom translated into terms with which the beginners can deal they remain largely meaningless. The children do appear to hear the word "Mexico" often enough to recognize it. Apparently many do gain a notion that Mexico refers to a place beyond their own, perhaps also encompassing their own community and the surrounding area. It is only the few children who continue their studies beyond the second and third grades who begin to have a concept of the Mexican nation and their place in it.

How successful are the schools at acculturating the children? Although there are many opportunities for the teachers to inculcate both the values and living styles of the national culture, little acculturation seems to take place except among the children who attend the centralized boarding schools of Ocosingo and Zinacantan. The students, most of them teenagers by the time they reach the upper grades, seem firmly rooted in their own cultures. Many of these more advanced students, themselves a small minority within their communities, have pursued their studies because they wish to acculturate, to avoid the traditional roles assigned to men and women, or to enjoy the wealth and prestige of being teachers themselves. Only on very rare occasions do they continue their schooling because of a love of academic learning and teaching. Yet few actually do acculturate while they remain in their own or in neighboring communities. It appears that is it only when they leave home, either to become teachers or to enter the ladino world of San Cristobal, that they take any major steps toward acculturation.

The schools have succeeded in breaking down some of the isolation of the Indians from the larger world. But as long as people remain in their own communities the schools can only supplement other efforts at acculturation and national integration.

Glossary

All words listed below are Spanish unless otherwise indicated. The INI transcription of Tzeltal and Tzotzil words has been used throughout and follows Spanish orthography. X is always pronounced like sh in English. The ' represents a glottal stop or click. Tzotzil and Tzeltal words are always accented on the last syllable.

achix (Tzeltal): Girl.
alal (Tzeltal): Baby.
alcaldes: Town officials.
antz (Tzeltal and Tzotzil): Woman.
atajadora: Ladina who waits at one of the entrances to San Cristobal to buy Indians' goods there and later sell them at the town market, usually at a considerable mark-up (literally, grabber).
atole: Cooked corn gruel.
ayuntamiento: Council of municipal officials.
baldaje: Peonage in which unpaid service to a landholder is exchanged for a house site, farm plot, and sometimes access to water.
baldío: Person living in baldaje.
barrio: Geographic division within a municipio.
bayan (Tzeltal): Many.
bik'it (Tzotzil): Little.
cabildo: Town hall.
caporal: Foreman.
casa chica: Euphemism for a mistress's home.
chanel (Tzotzil): Education or learning.
chenib (Tzotzil): Four.
chib (Tzotzil): Two.
chicha: Fermented sugar-water.
chijte': Tree with small narrow leaves that grows in profusion in the Highlands.
ch'in (Tzeltal): Little.
chixtot (Tzotzil): Species of small bird.
Ch'ulmetik (Tzotzil): Moon Goddess, the mother of Ch'ultotik; also identified with the Virgin Mary.
Ch'ultotik (Tzotzil): Sun God; also identified with Jesus Christ.
comal: Griddle placed over the open fire on which tortillas are baked.
compadrasco: Cogodparenthood; in mestizo communities it is given considerable importance and serves to extend familial ties to unrelated persons.
costal: Large burlap bag that can hold about 150 pounds of shelled corn.
curandero (-a): Shamanistic curer or faith healer.
encomienda: Feudal estate granted to a Spanish conqueror.
finca: Large farm or plantation.
gringo: North American; in Highland terms, anyone foreign to the State of Chiapas.
INI: National Indian Institute of Mexico (*Institúto Nacional Indigenista*).
jex (Tzotzil): Species of small bird.
jilol (Tzotzil): Shamanistic curer or faith healer.

jun (Tzeltal and Tzotzil):   One.
k'at'ix (Tzotzil):   Small, reddish fruit that grows wild in the Highland forests.
kerem (Tzeltal and Tzotzil):   Boy.
k'osh (Tzeltal and Tzotzil):   Spoiled youngest child of a family.
ladino (*-a*):   Mestizo native to the Chiapas Highlands.
litro: Liter.
machismo: Cult of exaggerated virility.
max (Tzotzil):   Monkey devil, an important role in several Chamula fiestas.
mayuk (Tzeltal):   None.
memelitas: Small, thick tortillas.
mestizo (*-a*):   Member of the Mexican national culture, itself a blend of Indian and Spanish elements.
milpa: Farm plot given over to subsistence agriculture, where corn and beans are the principal crops; some other vegetables are planted, and edible weeds are allowed to mature.
mis (Tzeltal):   Cat.
muk'tah (Tzotzil):   Big.
mukul (Tzeltal):   Big.
municipio: Municipality; politico-geographic area roughly equivalent to a county. In the Highlands many municipios correspond to Indian tribal regions, and the terms have come to be used somewhat interchangeably.
nene (Tzotzil):   Baby.
no'pel (Tzeltal):   Education or learning.
nopesel (Tzotzil):   Education or learning.
olol (Tzotzil):   Toddler.
oxib (Tzotzil):   Three.
paraje: Hamlet.
petate: Woven straw mat.
pijiji: Hopscotch game.
pomos (Tzotzil):   Species of plant that grows wild in the woods of Chamula.
porcelana: Ceramic bowl of conical shape that is wider than it is high; various sizes are often used as measures for items such as peanuts, small chiles, and so on.
poslom (Tzotzil):   Devil.
pozol: Uncooked corn gruel.
principal: Elder statesman and paraje leader.
promotor (*-es*):   Community development agent, bilingual teacher.
pukuj (Tzeltal and Tzotzil):   Devil.
pus (Tzeltal and Tzotzil):   Steam bathhouse.
quartilla: Dry measure equal to ¼ liter.
quartita: Small beer bottle, the smallest measure by which liquids such as kerosene and liquor are sold.
regidores: High-ranking town officials.
roña, la: Game of tag.
suplentes: Middle-ranking town officials.
sva'lej (Tzotzil):   Adolescent.
tablon: Amount of land a man should be able to weed in 6 to 8 hours (see *tarea*).
tamales: Steamed corn bread, often with a filling of beans or meat; Indian tamales are either plain or filled with beans.
tarea: Measure of agricultural work that an average man should be able to complete in about 6 to 8 hours; sometimes the actual amount of land a man should be able to weed in 6 to 8 hours; task.
ternas (Tzeltal):   Few.
tortilla: Flat, unleavened corn bread.
Totikshun (Tzotzil):   Sun God; also identified with Jesus Christ (see *Ch'ultotik*).

tseb (Tzotzil):   Girl.
unen (Tzotzil):   Toddler.
winik (Tzeltal and Tzotzil):   Man.
yiyel (Tzotzil):   Old.
zontle: Measure of 400.

Bibliography

Acción Indigenista, 1960, Number 79. (México, D.F.: Institúto Nacional Indigenista).

————, 1962, Number 108. (México, D.F.: Institúto Nacional Indigenista).

Adams, Don, and R. M. Bjork, 1969, *Education in Developing Areas*. New York: David McKay Company.

Anderson, C. C., 1949, "A Factorial Analysis of Reading." *British Journal of Educational Psychology* 19:220–221.

Anderson, Theodore, and M. Boyer, 1970, *Bilingual Schooling in the United States, Volume I*. Austin, Texas: Southwest Educational Development Laboratory.

Arias Sojob, Jacinto, 1969, personal communication.

————, 1970, Mexico's National Indian Institute and the Tzeltal–Tzotzil Co-ordinating Center. Unpublished manuscript.

Barrera-Vasquez, A., 1953, "The Tarascan Project in Mexico." In *The Use of Vernacular Languages in Education*. Paris: UNESCO, pp. 77–86.

Beeby, C. E., 1966, *The Quality of Education in Developing Countries*. Cambridge, Mass.: Harvard University Press.

Bender, Lauretta, 1946, *Bender Motor Gestalt Test Cards and Manual of Instructions*. New York: The Psychological Corporation.

Berbiers, John D., 1949, "Bilingualism in Belgium." *The Journal of Education* 81:210–212.

Bernstein, M. B., 1955, "Relationship between Interest and Reading Comprehension." *Journal of Educational Research* 49:283–288.

Blom, Franz, 1956, "The pre-Spanish Life of the Chiapas Indians of Today." In *Estudios Anthropologicos Publicados en Homenaje al Doctor Manuel Camio*. México, D.F.: pp. 277–285 (no publisher indicated).

Bloomfield, Leonard, 1933, *Language*. New York: Holt, Rinehart and Winston, Inc.

Boaz, Frank, 1889, "On Alternating Sounds." *American Anthropologist* 2:47–53.

Bovet, Pierre, 1934, "Bilingualism and Its Problems." In E. G. Malherbe, ed., *Educational Adaptations in a Changing Society*. Capetown and Johannesburg: Juta and Co., Ltd., 1937, pp. 81–86.

Brière, Eugène J., 1966, "An Investigation of Phonological Interference." *Language* 42:768–796.

Bruner, Jerome S., 1957, "On Perceptual Readiness." *Psychological Review* 64:123–152.

————, 1958, "Social Psychology and Perception," in J. F. Rosenblith and W. Allinsmith, eds., *The Causes of Behavior: Readings in Child Development and Educational Psychology*. Boston: Allyn and Bacon, Inc., 1962, pp. 363–369.

Buck, John N., 1948, "The H-T-P Technique: A Qualitative and Quantitative Scoring Manual." *Journal of Clinical Psychology*, Monograph Supplement 5.

Bumpass, Faye L., 1962, "Bridging the Gap between Oral Language Learning and Instruction in Reading for the Child Who Is Learning English as a Second Language." *The Reading Bulletin*, no. 112. Boston: Allyn and Bacon, Inc.

Burkhart, K. H., 1945, "An Analysis of Reading Ability." *Journal of Educational Research* 38:430–439.

Cancian, Frank, 1965, *Economics and Prestige in a Maya Community: The Religious Cargo System in Zinacantan*. Stanford, Calif.: Stanford University Press.

Caso, Alfonso, 1958, *Indigenismo*. México, D.F.: Institúto Nacional Indigenista.

144   BIBLIOGRAPHY

————, and others, 1964, *Realidades y Proyectos*. México, D.F.: Institúto Nacional Indigenista.

Castellanos, Manuel, 1970, personal communication.

Castro, Carlo A., 1959, *Los Hombres Verdaderos*. Xalapa, México: Universidad Veracruzana.

Castro de la Fuente, Angélica, 1955, "Teaching Spanish to Mexican Indians through the Vernacular," in *The Teaching of Modern Languages*. UNESCO, Problems in Education 10:281–287.

————, 1961, "La Alfabetización en Idiomas Indígenas y los Promotores Culturales," in *A William Cameran Townsend*. México, D.F.: Institúto Lingüístico de Verano.

Castro F., C. A., 1964, *Nuevo Programa de Educación para las Escuelas Primarias de la República Mexicana (detallado por meses)*. México, D.F.: Ediciones Avante.

Colby, Benjamin N., 1959a, A Field Sketch of Some Recurring Themes in Zinacantecan Culture. San Cristóbal de Las Casas, México: Biblioteca Fray Bartolomé. Unpublished manuscript.

————, 1959b, Culture Change and Education in Chiapas. San Cristóbal de Las Casas, México: Biblioteca Fray Bartolomé. Unpublished manuscript.

————, 1961, "Indian Attitudes toward Education and Inter-ethnic Contact in Mexico." *Practical Anthropology* 8 (March–April):77–85.

————, and P. van ·den Berghe, 1961, "Ethnic Relations in Southeastern Mexico." *American Anthropologist* 63:772–792.

Collier, George A., and V. Bricker, 1970, "Nicknames and Social Structure in Zinacantan." *American Anthropologist* 72:289–302.

Consejo Nacional Técnico de la Educación, 1962, *Reforma Educativa*. México, D.F.: Secretaría de Educación Pública.

Cruz Santiago, Jaime, 1971, Desarrollo y Programación del Centro Coordinador Indigenista Tzeltal–Tzotzil, Dependencia del INI. Unpublished manuscript.

Darcy, N. T., 1952, "The Performance of Bilingual Puerto Rican Children on Verbal and Non-language Tests of Intelligence." *Journal of Educational Research* 45:499–506.

————, 1953, "A Review of the Literature on the Effects of Bilingualism upon the Measurements of Intelligence." *Journal of Genetic Psychology* 82:21–57.

Dart, Francis E., 1963, "The Rub of Cultures." *Foreign Affairs* 41:360–371.

Davis, Frederick B., 1944, "Fundamental Factors of Comprehension in Reading." *Psychometrika* 9:185–197.

————, 1956, "The Teaching of Comprehension of Reading in the Secondary School." *Education* 76:541–544.

de la Fuente, Julio, 1940, "Ocho Años de Experiencia en el Medio Rural." *Revista Mexicana de Educación* 1(Agosto):57–67.

————, 1958, Relaciones Etnicas en los Altos de Chiapas. San Cristóbal de Las Casas, México: Biblioteca Fray Bartolomé. Unpublished manuscript.

Domínguez Aguirre, Carmen, and Enriquetta León Gonzales, 1962, *Mi Libro y Mi Cuaderno de Trabajo de Primer Año—Instructivo para el Maestro*. México, D.F.: Comisión Nacional de los Libros de Textos Gratuitos.

Doob, Leonard W., 1957, "The Effect of Language on Verbal Expression and Recall." *American Anthropologist* 59:88–100.

————, 1959, "Psychological Factors in Community Education," in N. B. Henry, ed., *Community Education, Principles and Practices from World-wide Experience, Fifty-eighth Yearbook of the National Society for the Study of Education*. Chicago: University of Chicago Press, pp. 97–121.

Drucker, Susana, 1963, *Cambio de Indumentaria*. México, D.F.: Institúto Nacional Indigenista.

Epperson, David C., and R. A. Schmuck, 1963, "The Uses of Social Psychology in Comparative Education." *Comparative Education Review* 6:182–190.

Fantz, Robert L., 1961, "The Origin of Form Perception." *Scientific American* 204 (5):66–72.

Fearing, Franklin, 1954, "An examination of the conceptions of Benjamin Whorf in the light of theories of cognition and perception," in H. Hoijer, ed., *Language in Culture.* Chicago: University of Chicago Press, pp. 47–81.

Fife, Robert H., and H. T. Manuel, 1951, *The Teaching of English in Puerto Rico.* San Juan, Puerto Rico: Department of Education Press.

Finley, Carmen J., 1963, "A Comparison of the California Achievement Test, Metropolitan Achievement Test, and Iowa Test of Basic Skills." *California Journal of Educational Research* 14:79–88.

Flores, Ana Maria, and others, 1961, *Fundamento Estadístico del Plan de Once Años de Educación Primaria.* México, D.F.: Secretaría de Indústria y Comercio, Departamento de Muestreo.

Fogelquist, Donald F., 1950, "The Bilingualism of Paraguay." *Hispania* 33:23–27.

Frostig, Marianne, W. Lefever, and J. R. B. Whittlesey, 1961, "Scoring and Evaluation Booklet for Marianne Frostig Developmental Test of Visual Perception." Unpublished manuscript.

———, 1963, "The Marianne Frostig Developmental Test of Visual Perception, 1962 Standardization." Unpublished manuscript.

Gallo M., Victor, and D. Gutíerrez, 1963, *Edificios, Anexos y Mobilario.* México, D.F.: Institúto Federal de Capacitación del Magisterio. Mimeographed paper.

Garcia Ruíz, Ramón, 1963, *Princípios y Técnica de la Supervisión Escolar.* México, D.F.: Institúto Federal de Capacitación del Magisterio.

Gonzales, Oscar M., 1965, personal communication.

Gossen, Gary, 1969, personal communication.

Gray, William S., 1956, *The Teaching of Reading and Writing: An International Survey.* Paris: UNESCO, and Chicago: Scott, Foresman and Company.

———, 1959, "World literacy: Its status and problems," in N. B. Henry, ed., *Community Education Principles and Practices from World-wide Experience, Fifty-eighth Yearbook of the National Society for the Study of Education.* Chicago: University of Chicago Press, pp. 122–146.

Greenberg, Joseph H., 1954, "Concerning inferences from linquistic to nonlinguistic data," in H. Hoijer, ed., *Language in Culture.* Chicago: University of Chicago Press, pp. 3–19.

Greenfield, Patricia M., 1970, personal communication.

Grieve, D. W., and A. Taylor, 1952, "Media of Instruction: A Preliminary Study of the Relative Merits of English and an African Vernacular as Teaching Media." *Gold Coast Education* 1:36–52.

Guiteras-Holmes, Calixta, 1948, "Organización Social de Tseltales y Tzotziles, México." *América Indígena* 8:46–62.

———, 1961, *Perils of the Soul.* New York: The Free Press of Glencoe.

Hall, W. E., and F. P. Robinson, 1945, "An Analytic Approach to the Study of Reading Skill." *Journal of Educational Psychology* 36:429–442.

Harcourt, Brace & World, Inc., 1962, *Correlations between Stanford and Metropolitan Measures of Achievement for Pupils in Grades Two through Nine in a New England System.* New York: Harcourt, Brace and World, Inc., Test Department. Mimeographed manuscript.

Harrison, Selig S., 1957, *The Most Dangerous Decades: An Introduction to the Comparative Study of Language Policy in Multilingual States.* New York: Language and Communication Research Center, Columbia University.

Haugan, Einar, 1956, "The bilingual individual," in S. Saporta and J. R. Bastian, eds., *Psycholinguistics, A Book of Readings.* New York: Holt, Rinehart and Winston, Inc., pp. 395–407.

Henry, Jules, 1960, "A Cross-Cultural Outline of Education." *Current Anthropology* 1 (July):267–305.

Holland, William R., 1963, *Medicina Maya en los Altos de Chiapas.* México, D.F.: Institúto Naciónal Indigenista. D. Cazes, trans.

Holmes, Jack A., 1954, "Factors Underlying Major Reading Disabilities at the College Level." *Genetic Psychology Monographs* 49:3–95.

Institúto Federal de Capacitación del Magisterio, 1963, *Teoria y aplicación de la Reforma Educativa.* México, D.F.: Secretaría de Educación Pública.

———, 1964. *Guías de Estudio y Actividades.* México, D.F.: Secretaría de Educación Pública.

Jahoda, Gustav, 1961, "Aspects of Westernization: A Study of Adult-Class Students in Ghana: I." *British Journal of Sociology* 12:375–386.

Jan-Tausch, James, 1962, "Concrete Thinking as a Factor in Reading Comprehension," in J. A. Figuere, ed., *Challenge and Experiment in Reading. International Reading Association Conference Proceedings* 7:161–164.

Jones, W. R., 1952, "The Language Handicap of Welsh-speaking Children." *British Journal of Educational Psychology* 22:114–123.

Judd, C. H., and G. T. Buswell, 1922, "Silent Reading: A Study of the Various Types," in *Supplementary Educational Monographs No. 23.* Chicago: University of Chicago Press.

Kreusler, A., 1961, "Bilingualism in Soviet Non-Russian Schools." *Elementary School Journal* 62 (Nov.):94–99.

Lado, Robert, 1957, *Linguistics across Cultures: Applied Linguistics for Teachers.* Ann Arbor: University of Michigan Press.

Lambert, W. E., and others, 1961, *Attitudinal and Cognitive Aspects of Intensive Study of a Second Language.* Montreal: McGill University. Mimeographed paper.

———, J. Havelka, and C. Crosby, 1958, "The Influence of Language-Acquisition Contexts on Bilingualism," in S. Saporta and R. Bastian, eds., *Psycholinguistics, A Book of Readings.* New York: Holt, Rinehart and Winston, Inc., pp. 407–414.

Langsam, R. T., 1941, "A Factorial Analysis of Reading Ability." *Journal of Experimental Education* 10:57–63.

Maccoby, Michael, 1958, The NYDO test. Personal communication.

Malherbe, Ernest G., 1943, *The Bilingual School: A Study of Bilingualism in South Africa.* Johannesburg: Bilingual School Association. (Also published: London: Longmans, Green and Co., 1946.)

——— (ed.), 1937, *Educational Adaptations in a Changing Society: Report of the South African Education Conference Held in Capetown and Johannesburg in July, 1934, under the Auspices of the New Education Fellowship.* Capetown and Johannesburg: Juta and Co., Ltd.

Maroquín, Alejandro D., 1955, *Consideraciónes sobre el Problema Económica de la Región Tzeltal–Tzotzil.* México, D.F.: Institúto Nacional Indigenista.

Mead, Margaret, 1959, "Cultural Factors in Community Education Programs," in N. B. Henry, ed., *Community Education Principles and Practices from Worldwide Experience, Fifty-eighth Yearbook of the National Society for the Study of Education.* Chicago: University of Chicago Press, pp. 66–96.

Metzger, Barbara, 1958, An Ethnographic Summary of Zinacantan. San Cristóbal de Las Casas, México: Biblioteca Fray Bartolomé. Unpublished manuscript.

———, 1960, Notes on the History of Indian–Ladino Relations in Chiapas. San Cristóbal de Las Casas, México: Biblioteca Fray Bartolomé. Mimeographed paper.

Modiano, Nancy, 1966a, *A Comparative Study of Two Approaches to the Teaching of Reading in the National Language.* Final Report, Cooperative Research Project S–237, U. S. Department of Health, Education and Welfare, Office of Education.

———, 1966b, Reading Comprehension in the National Language: A Comparative Study of Bilingual and All-Spanish Approaches to Reading Instruction in Selected Indian Schools in the Highlands of Chiapas, Mexico. Doctoral dissertation, New York University.

Montes Sanchez, Fidencio, 1954, *Guía del Promotor.* San Cristóbal de Las Casas, México: Institúto Nacional Indigenista.

Morrison, J. C., 1958, *The Puerto Rican Study, 1953–1957: A Report on the Education and Adjustment of Puerto Rican Pupils in the Public Schools of the City of New York.* New York: Board of Education, City of New York.

Nash, June, 1959, Social Structure and Social Organization in Oxchuc, Chiapas. San Cristóbal de Las Casas, México: Biblioteca Fray Bartolomé. Unpublished manuscript.

———, 1970, *In the Eyes of the Ancestors.* New Haven, Conn.: Yale University Press.

Orata, Pedro T., 1953, "The Iloila Experiment in Education through the Vernacular," in *The Use of Vernacular Languages in Education.* Paris: UNESCO, pp. 123–131.

Paz Sarza, Leonardo, 1964, personal communication.

Perkins, James A., 1967, "Final Report of Conference Chairmen: The International Conference on the World Crisis in Education." *Bulletin on International Education* 5:3–8.

Piaget, Jean, and B. Inhelder, 1969, *The Psychology of the Child.* New York: Basic Books.

Platten, G. J., and others, 1953, *The Use of the Vernacular in Teaching in the South Pacific.* South Pacific Commission Technical Paper no. 44. Nourmea, New Caledonia, and Sydney, Australia: South Pacific Commission.

Pozas, Ricardo, 1959a, *Chamula, un Pueblo de los Altos de Chiapas.* México, D.F.: Institúto Nacional Indigenista.

———, 1959b, *Juan Perez Jolote: Biografía de un Tzotzil.* México, D.F.: Fondo de Cultura Económica.

Ramírez, Rafael, n.d., *Como Dar a México un Idioma.* México, D.F.: Secretaría de Educación Pública.

Redfield, R., and A. Villa Rojas, 1939, "Notes on the Ethnography of Tzeltal Communities in Chiapas," in *Contributions to American Anthropology and History No. 78.* Washington, D.C.: Carnegie Institution of Washington, D.C.

Remesal, Fray A. de, 1908, *1619 Historia de la Provincia de S. Vicente de Chiapas y Guatemala.* Madrid.

Robey, John S., 1969, personal communication.

Romano, Augustín, 1964, "Educación," in *Realidades y Proyectos.* México, D.F.: Institúto Nacional Indigenista.

Rosenthal, Robert, 1966, *Experimenter Effects in Behavioral Research.* New York: Appleton–Century–Crofts.

Ruíz, Ramon E., 1963, *Mexico: The Challenge of Illiteracy and Poverty.* San Marino, California: The Huntington Library.

Santiago, Filiberto, 1965, personal communication.

Santiago Montes, Andres, 1965, personal communication.

Sapir, Edward, 1925, "Sound Patterns in Language." *Language* 1:37–51.

Sauer, Charles A., 1943, "The Place of the Vernacular Language in Colonial Education." *Modern Language Journal* 27:180–183.

Schwartz, A. A., and I. H. Rosenberg, 1955, "Observations on the Significance of Animal Drawings." *American Journal of Orthopsychiatry* 25:729–746.

Secretaría de Educación Pública, 1961a, *Instructivo, Escuela Rural.* México, D.F.: Secretaría de Educación Pública.

———, 1961b, *Programas de Educación Primarias Aprobados por el Consejo Nacional Técnico de la Educación.* México, D.F.: Secretaría de Educación Pública.

———, 1963, *Report on the Educational Movement in Mexico, 1962–1963, XXVI International Conference of Public Instruction.* México, D.F.: Ediciones Oasis, S.A.

———, 1964, *Plan de Educación Indígena para 1964.* Mimeographed paper.

Secretaría de Indústria y Comercio, 1968, *Anuario Estadístico de los Estados Unidos Mexicanos 1966–1967.* México, D.F.: Secretaría de Indústria y Comercio.

Segall, Marshall H., D. T. Campbell, and M. Herskovitz, 1966, *The Influence of Culture on Visual Perception.* New York: Bobbs–Merrill.

Serduchenko, G. P., 1962, "The Eradication of Illiteracy and the Creation of New Written Languages in the USSR." *International Journal of Adult and Youth Education* 14:23–29.

Siverts, Henning, 1956, "Social and Cultural Changes in a Tzeltal (Mayan) Municipio, Chiapas, Mexico," in *Proceedings of the Thirty-second International Congress of Americanists.* Copenhagen: Munksgaard, pp. 177–189, 1958.

Slocum, M. C., 1956, "Cultural Changes among the Oxchuc Tzeltals. In *Estudios Antropológicos Publicados en Homenaje al Doctor Manuel Gamio.* México, D.F.: pp. 491–495 (no publisher indicated).

Smith, Henry E., and E. V. Dechant, 1961, *Psychology in Teaching Reading.* Englewood Cliffs, N.J.: Prentice-Hall, Inc.

Smith, M. E., 1957, "Progress in the Use of English after Twenty-two Years by Children of Chinese Ancestry in Honolulu." *Journal of Genetic Psychology* 90:255–258.

———, and L. M. Kardon, 1961, "Progress in the Use of English after Twenty Years by Children of Filipino and Japanese Ancestry in Hawaii." *Journal of Genetic Psychology* 99:129–138.

Soffetti, J. P., 1960, "Bilingualism and Biculturalism." *Modern Language Journal* 44:275–277.

Spaulding, Seth, J. Singleton, and P. Watson, 1968, "The Context of International Development Education." *Review of Educational Research* 38:201–212.

Swadesh, Mauricio, 1960, "Problemas Sociales y Lingüísticos en la Castellanización," in *Seminario de Estudios Antropológicos, Mesa Redonda sobre Factores Sociales, Lingüísticos y Pedagógicos en la Castellanización y Alfabetización de Indígenas.* México, D.F.: (no publisher indicated).

Thorndike, Edward L., 1917, "Reading as Reasoning: A Study of Mistakes in Paragraph Reading." *Journal of Educational Psychology* 8:323–332.

Tireman, Lloyd S., 1948, *Teaching Spanish-speaking Children.* Albuquerque: The University of New Mexico Press.

Thurlbeck, W., 1934, "The medium question," in E. G. Malherbe, ed., *Educational Adaptations in a Changing Society.* Capetown and Johannesburg: Juta and Co., Ltd., pp. 470–471.

Torres-Bodet, Jaime, 1961, *Programas de Educación Primaria Aprobados por el Consejo Nacional Técnico de la Educación* (Tercera edición). México, D.F.: Secretaría de Educación Pública.

Trens, Manuel, 1957, *Historia de Chiapas: Desde los Tiempos Mas Remotos Hasta la Caida del Segundo Imperio, I* (Segunda edición). México, D.F.: (no publisher indicated).

UNESCO, 1953, "The Use of Vernacular Languages in Education." *Monographs on Fundamental Education VIII*, Paris.

———, 1957, "World Illiteracy at Mid-century." *Monographs on Fundamental Education XI*, Paris.

———, 1958, *World Survey of Education II: Primary Education*. Paris.

Villareal C., Tomas, 1962, *Los Nuevos Programas de Educación Primaria y Su Realización*. México, D.F.: Institúto Federal de Capacitación del Magisterio.

Villa Rojas, Alfonso, 1947, *Notas sobre la Etnografía de los Indios Tzeltales de Oxchuc, Chiapas, Mexico*. University of Chicago Microfilm Collection of Manuscripts on Middle American Cultural Anthropology, no. 7.

———, 1959, "La Zona Tzeltal–Tzotzil: Su Configuración Social y Cultural. *Acción Indigenista*, Number 72.

Vogt, Evon Z., 1969, *Zinacantan: A Maya Community in the Highlands of Chiapas*. Cambridge, Mass.: Harvard University Press.

Weinreich, Uriel, 1953, *Languages in Contact*. New York: Linguistic Circle of New York.

West, Michael, 1926, *Bilingualism, with Special Reference to Bengal*. Occasional reports, No. 13, Bureau of Education, India. Calcutta: Government of India Central Publications Branch.

———, 1936, "The Language Problem and the Teaching of English in Puerto Rico." Unpublished report for the Commissioner of Education of Puerto Rico.

Whorf, Benjamin L., 1939, "The Relation of Habitual Thought and Behavior to Language," in J. B. Carroll, ed., *Language, Thought, and Reality: Selected Writings of Benjamin Lee Whorf*. New York: John Wiley and Sons, Inc., 1956.

Wolf, Eric, 1959, *Sons of the Shaking Earth*. Chicago: University of Chicago Press, Phoenix Books, 1962.

Wolff, Hans, 1950, "Partial Comparison of Sound Systems of English and Puerto Rican Spanish." *Language Learning* 3:38–41.

Recommended reading

Cancian, Frank, 1965, *Economics and Prestige in a Maya Community: The Religious Cargo System in Zinacantan.* Stanford, Calif.: Stanford University Press.
An examination of the relationship between male prestige roles and economic productivity in Zinacantan.
————, 1972, *Change and Uncertainty in a Peasant Economy: The Maya Corn Farmers of Zinacantan.* Stanford, Calif.: Stanford University Press.
A thorough study of the economic base of Zinacantecan life.
Castro, Carlo Antonio, 1959, *Los Hombres Verdaderos.* Xalapa, México: Universidad Veracruzana.
A novel based on the lives of the first INI teachers in Oxchuc.
Hilger, Inez M., 1966, *Field Guide to the Ethnological Study of Child Life.* Revised edition. New Haven: Human Relations Area Files Press.
An excellent field guide for the study of children and child rearing.
Nash, June, 1970, *In the Eyes of the Ancestors: Belief and Behavior in a Mayan Community.* New Haven: Yale University Press.
An excellent description of life and belief in the Tzeltal community of Amatenango del Valle.
Pozas, Ricardo, 1962, *Juan the Chamula.* Berkeley: University of California Press. Translated by Lysander Kemp.
The biography of a former president of Chamula.
Siverts, Henning, 1969, *Oxchuc: Una Tribu Maya de México.* Mexico City: Institúto Indigenista Interamericano.
An ethnography of Oxchuc, with special attention to social and political organization.
Vogt, Evon Z., 1970, The *Zinacantecos of Mexico: A Modern Maya Way of Life.* New York: Holt, Rinehart and Winston, Inc.
A detailed study of life in Zinacantan, a Tzotzil community, with special attention to social organization and religion.
Wilson, Carter, 1965, *Crazy February.* Philadelphia: J. B. Lippincott Company.
A novel based on the life and peoples of Chamula, the largest Tzotzil community in Chiapas.
Wolf, Eric, 1962, *Sons of the Shaking Earth.* Chicago: University of Chicago Press, Phoenix Books.
An excellent social history of Mexico and Guatemala from the time of the Spanish conquest to the 1950s.